THE IMPORTANCE OF SIBLING RELATIONSHIPS IN PSYCHOANALYSIS

THE IMPORTANCE OF SIBLING RELATIONSHIPS IN PSYCHOANALYSIS

By

Prophecy Coles

KARNAC

LONDON   NEW YORK

Published in 2003 by
H. Karnac (Books) Ltd.
6 Pembroke Buildings, London NW10 6RE

Reprinted 2003

British Library Cataloguing in Publication Data

A C.I.P. for this book is available from the British Library

   ISBN 1 85575 923 3

Edited, designed, and produced by The Studio Publishing Services Ltd,
Exeter EX4 8JN

Printed and bound in Great Britain by
Biddles Ltd, Guildford and King's Lynn

10 9 8 7 6 5 4 3 2

www.karnacbooks.com

For Walter, our sons and our grandchildren.

Thus rambling we were schooled in deepest lore,
And learned the meaning that give words a soul,
The fear, the love, the primal passionate store,
Whose shaping impulses make manhood whole.

Brother and Sister, George Eliot (1896)

CONTENTS

ACKNOWLEDGEMENTS

I thank those patients who have consented to my use of their material. I am indebted to Patrick Casement, Tanya Coles, Geoffrey Elkan, Melanie Hart, Kirsty Hall, Bob Hinshelwood, Estelle Roith, Ann Scott, Joseph Schwartz, and Jennifer Silverstone who have made important contributions to my thinking. I thank Graham Sleight for his suggestion that I write this book. My own siblings are remembered, as are my children and their children. Finally, this book could not have been written without the support and encouragement of my husband, Walter.

Prophecy Coles is a psychoanalytic psychotherapist in private practice in London. She trained at the Lincoln Centre for Psychotherapy and has written several papers, including a study on the Armenian painter Arshile Gorky, and clinical papers on eating disorders, sexual perversions, female sexuality and siblings.

Introduction

W hen I told a friend that I was writing a book on siblings, he said that one of his earliest and most tender memories was being taken out to tea by his mother to a Lyons Corner House. "I am sure my elder brother would have been there, but I have no memory of this," he said. In some ways that vignette captures the theme of this book. Where have our siblings gone? Why do they not feature as significant figures in psychoanalytic accounts of the inner world?

I believe that there is a tendency in us all to wish that we could be the only child. The only one having tea with our mother. We hold fantasies that this would be a world without conflict, a world in which we would inherit all our parents' possessions. We would know, more surely, that we were the most loved child. Iris Murdoch, who was an only child, is quoted by Conradi (2001) as saying, "My mother and father and I were always three, and we were always happy ... 'a perfect trinity of love'." (p. 33). Psychoanalytical theory seems to have colluded with the wish to be the only child, though it may be more sceptical about the belief in a "perfect trinity of love". Siblings are scarcely mentioned in the literature and the concept of a sibling transference does not appear in any of the psychoanalytic dictionaries. In some ways the concentration on the oedipal triad is a more comfortable position, as is the memory of my friend with his mother in the Lyons Corner Shop.

I hope to show that the emphasis upon the Oedipus complex, as the fulcrum of our psychic development, is an oversimplification. It is clear from the myth itself that, if we give Oedipus the central role in psychic development, we do not need siblings. Oedipus had none that figured in his dilemma and therefore we do not need to include them in a theory of our neuroses. I do not dismiss the idea that we all believe, at times, that the world would be a better place without the intrusion of siblings, nor do I want to ignore the crucial importance of parents in the emotional life of the child. But I do believe that this is only half the story of our emotional development. We need our siblings and peers to help us get away from our parents and teach us how to relate in a different way. I shall also be suggesting that it is too simple to see the relationships we create with our siblings as a displacement from parental ones. The fact that, in some cases, this may be true does not provide sufficient reason to claim this is true in all cases. The feelings we have towards our siblings have an important place in the complexity of our emotional life, and to dismiss their significance is to impoverish our internal world.

One of the questions I shall be raising is whether we fear the power of sibling relationships. Are they more passionate than parental relationships? Do we "work through them" and separate from them in the same way as with parents? Psychoanalytic orthodoxy seems to have accepted Freud's view that all sibling relationships are based upon "primal hatred", "the unfathomably deep hostility ... (the) death wish, (the) intent to murder" (Fliess, 1956, p. 8).[1]

By contrast, George Eliot, Dorothy and William Wordsworth, and Melanie Klein experienced deep passionate love for their siblings, and yet their experiences have been ignored within psychoanalytic theory, except as a "transformation" (*ibid.*) of their "primal hatred". It is an interesting paradox that we seem to have implicitly accepted Freud's belief in the "primal hatred" of siblings while at the same time dismissing the importance of siblings in the inner world.

Several emotional and intellectual strands interweave throughout this book. In the first place, I believe that my relationships with my siblings have deeply affected the way I relate to my contemporaries. I have found little intellectual support for such an idea within the psychoanalytic literature in the U.K. Mitchell's book *Mad Men and Medusa* (2000) is the first book of significance to redress the dearth of thinking about siblings. She claims that there has been "a massive repression of the significance of all the love and hate of sibling relationship and their heirs in marital affinity and friendships" (p. 77) and I completely endorse such a view. However, Mitchell and I disagree about the nature of the sibling relationship, as I shall be arguing in Chapter Eight.

I stand as an object-relation theorist, and hold the view that we cannot understand our psychic life without the presence of others. I am unable intellectually to defend the concept of a death drive, though I believe all of us can be self-destructive. And I do not hold that our psychic existence is predicated upon absence, loss, and destructiveness, even though these are undoubtedly universal experiences. I have never known a baby who I would want to describe as having been born with an "excess of object hostility" (Britton, 1998). It is truer to the way I see the world to imagine that we are all born with the capacity to love and respond to the world, and it is the deformation of that capacity, through the hazards of experience, that bring people to our consulting room.

It will be seen that I place the role of experience as crucial in understanding the inner life. I have taken siblings as real events whose existence, in the first place, shapes our inner world and, therefore, the emphasis throughout the book has been to pay less attention to the influence of the inner fantasies upon the way siblings are experienced. This has been a deliberate intention on my part. It needs to be accepted that, if we have siblings, they play a significant part in our emotional and sexual development. Only when we have found a way of incorporating them into our theories about the structure of the inner world, will we need a much fuller account of the fantasies that surround siblings than I have given.

Another of my basic assumptions is that the psychoanalytic exploration of the mind stands on the margin between a science of the mind and a philosophy of the mind. Schwartz argued,

Historically psychoanalysis is located within the traditions of Western science as a systematic attempt to understand an aspect of human experience of the world—in this case, our experience of our own personal inner world. [1999, p. 2]

The uneasy alliance between a tradition of Western science and the pursuit of understanding of the "personal inner world" still causes conflict in psychoanalytic epistemology. What is the nature of the knowledge that psychoanalysis postulates? If we take the arguments of the few theoreticians who have been interested in siblings, they are extraordinarily divergent. Freud seems to have found his relationship with his siblings difficult (Anzieu, 1986; Gay, 1988; Jones, 1953) and we find a theory that siblings are fundamentally hated rivals. Klein, on the other hand, seems to have loved her brother (Grosskurth, 1985), and we have a theory about the importance of sibling love. This disparity of views has led me to the belief that, though the aspiration in psychoanalysis is to find a systematic and scientific theory of the workings of the unconscious mind, when we read the great creative writers of psychoanalysis, such as Freud and Klein, we are primarily listening to the complex workings of their own minds. Some of these theories have permeated their way into our culture and have altered the way we conceive our minds. Whether we like it or not we live in a post-Freudian world, and this may be said to testify to the "truth" of psychoanalysis. I want to suggest that the "truth" of these ideas rests upon the fact that they are true expressions of the writer's personal feelings. When Freud writes, "All my friends have in a certain sense been re-incarnations of the first figure (John)" (1900a, p. 483), he is describing a truth about himself. Similarly, when Klein writes, "the existence of sexual relations between children, especially between brothers and sisters ... may influence the child's general development favourably" (1932, pp. 118–119), she is writing from her own experience. Are they universal truths? Clearly not, and yet we are moved and struck by them. This leads me to suggest that autobiography plays a crucial and invaluable part in psychoanalytic theory and should not be severed from it. Or, to put it the other way round, psychoanalytic theory may be the theorization of autobiography.[2] I am taking autobiography to mean the search for insight into the self, rather than the rationalization of our peculiarities.[3] This way of thinking seems to suggest that psychoanalysis is neither a science nor a philosophy of the mind and that its claim to knowledge lies alongside the imaginative reconstructions of great literature and autobiography.[4]

As a result of the continuity I make between great literature and psychoanalysis, I have used literary sources to illustrate my argument when I have not been able to find clinical material. This raises questions about how I am reading these texts. I do not believe a literary text is the same as a clinical study, for the intention behind the writing must be different. Nevertheless, when I use George Eliot I do so because I believe she had enormous psychological insight and understood the power of the unconscious mind. In *The Mill on the Floss* (1860), George Eliot helps us to see and think about the richness and complexity of sibling relationships in ways that few clinical texts have shown. I have also compared Dunmore's and Johnston's literary excursions into incest for they seem to have illuminated a psychological insight that is not to be found in any case studies that I have read. We have been warned by Kate Springford and George Craig (2001) that the psychoanalysing of literary characters is not illuminating for a literary text. I do, however, think that a literary text can illuminate those areas that we, as psychotherapists, have been unable to see. I have to leave the reader to decide whether I have distorted the intention of the writers whose work I use.

I need to acknowledge all that I have left out that concerns sibling relationships. I have only touched on the effect of sibling order,[5] and I have neglected a full discussion of the effect of sibling death on the remaining children. I have not looked at sibling relationships and their link with parental fantasies that may have been projected onto the children (Laplanche, 1989, 1999). Cases where there is an only child or twins have been ignored in the body of my text.

I chose to leave out the only child as my interest has been in beginning to describe the effect of sibling *relationships* upon the psyche. Moreover, I have seen few only children in my practice, and this in itself may be a significant fact. Are only children better protected from the conflicts that bring people into therapy? Or is it the case that the only child still represents a small minority in the U.K.? I am aware that there is a qualitative difference in the feel of the inner world of only children compared to those who have siblings. Iris Murdoch was an only child and she "began writing stories at nine in order to provide herself with imaginary siblings" (Conradi, 2001, p. 46). This is not unique to only children. Many children with siblings invent an imaginary companion to compensate for the disappointment and pain of unsuccessful sibling attachments (Nagera, 1969). However, the child who invents an imaginary sibling has a companion that is "under the absolute control of its creator" (Volkan & Ast, 1997, p. 107). This is not true for a child who has an actual sibling in the external world.

The only child, as well as the child with siblings, has to face the nature and fantasy of the sexual intimacy of the parents. For the only child one question will be, "why no more siblings?" For the child with siblings the question might be "why more?" But I would not want to assert that the structure of the psyche is altered by these variables. What is different between an only child and a child with siblings is the *texture* of their inner world. By that I mean, there is much more "noise" in the inner world of someone who has several siblings. In my experience, the inner world of an only child is quieter, their dreams are less populated by events with a lot of people and the transference experience is different. The intense jealousy about being displaced by a sibling can never be compared to the rivalry of children at nursery school and, therefore, only children are protected from a particular type of jealousy, sibling jealousy. To give an example, I have known patients who have had an immediate transference experience of being robbed of my attention if I mention the name of their sibling. This acute experience is unique to that of siblings and is well described by Mitchell (2000) as a fear of being annihilated by the other. I am not saying that the only child cannot have existential anxieties, but what I am saying is that the aetiology is going to be different. Putting it the other way round, if a patient has severe existential anxieties, and one discovers that he or she may have had an overwhelming experience of sibling rivalry, then that experience needs to be taken into account in any theoretical formulation and understanding.

I have not considered twins, primarily because I have had no experience of working with twins. There is a rich literature on the twin in fact and fantasy. Twins have a particular and important place in culture and mythology, such as the tale of Jacob and Esau. In psychoanalytic theory, we see clinical papers on the effect of being a twin (Abraham, 1950; Burlingham, 1951; Glenn, 1966), while there are others that deal with the fantasy of having a twin (Burlingham, 1945; Nagera, 1969). In some theories, they are described as rivals from the moment of conception and believed to have fought in the womb and come into the world hating each other. There are other accounts that take an opposite view and suggest that twins can live in harmony with each other (Piontelli, 1992). A more literary version of the twin relationship suggests they can represent a "sublime fusion of two beings" (Luzes, 1990, p. 99).

This book concentrates upon families where there is more than one child, and I have developed my argument in the following way. In Chapter One, I distinguish between a sibling transference and a parent/child transference and illustrate, with clinical material, the interweaving of the developmental strands between the two types of transference. In Chapter Two, I introduce Freud's view on siblings and address the question as to why siblings have been ignored in psychoanalytic theory. In Chapter Three, I link Freud's neglect of siblings to his experience of his own siblings. This is followed in Chapter Four by a critique of Freud's treatment of "The Wolfman". I argue that the relationship of "The Wolfman" and his sister cannot be ignored in understanding his pathology and I, furthermore, suggest that the case illuminates Freud's own personal discovery of the meaning of the primal scene. In Chapter Five, I turn to early Klein for a more fulsome picture of the impact of sibling relationships on the developing psyche and, most importantly, the idea that it is through identification with our siblings that adult heterosexuality is achieved. In Chapter Six, I turn to the question of sibling incest, a problem raised by Klein in the previous chapter. Why does sibling incest occur, is it more frequent than parent/child incest and is it less damaging? In Chapter Seven the concept of identification with siblings is further explored via the concept of brotherly love. Anna Freud and Sophie Dann's observation of six war-orphaned children emphasizes the importance of sibling/peer relationships in mental health. In Chapter Eight I address the question of how we might think about the sibling experience and what makes it different from the parent/child relationship. Chapter Nine is the conclusion.

Notes

1. I would like to thank Darian Leader for sending me this quotation.
2. While revising this text for publication I read Gubrich-Simitis (2002) On "Die Traumdeutung". In this article she explores the reasons for the revisions and additions which Freud made to this book, throughout his lifetime. She suggests that he was conflicted between his knowledge that it was a work of "... my own self analysis, my reaction to my father's death" (Freud, 1900a, p. 25) and his wish for his theory of dream interpretation to be considered a science of the human subject.
3. I am grateful to Richard Wollheim for pointing out the need to make this distinction.
4. The idea that we can understand the mind of man through his imagination stems from a much neglected eighteenth-century thinker Giambattista Vico. In 1728 he wrote his *Autobiography* (1963). He suggested that man can only come to know his mind by discovering his own autobiography. If an individual can come to understand how his beliefs have come about and trace the development of these beliefs, then something else happens within the mind. He can claim to have "true" knowledge. "The rule and criterion of truth is to have made it. We can know nothing that we have not made." This idea did not lead into a solipsistic world of individuals unable to understand each other or agree. On the contrary, he held a passionate belief in certain universal truths that united man. These were spelt out in his later work *The New Science* (1975) in which he wrote of a "common mental language" (p. 161) that concerned itself with religious beliefs, sexual relationships, and the burying of the dead. This common mental language, nevertheless, was subject to evolutionary change as man's ideas developed (Coles, 1975).
5. Freud was the eldest of his family. Melanie Klein was the youngest in hers. George Eliot was the second in her family. The sibling position may be the most important factor in determining the way we conceive the world.

CHAPTER ONE

The sibling transference

I t is rare to find a psychoanalytic book on theory or technique in which siblings play a part in the way the internal world is conceived. There are a few publications, (Agger, 1988; Bank & Kahn, 1997; Colonna & Newman, 1983; Mitchell, 2000; Sharpe & Rosenblatt, 1994) in which, with the exception of Mitchell, the work has been centred in the U.S. There is little reference to the concept of a sibling transference in the analytic journals and when it is mentioned, it is analysed as a displaced oedipal transference.

I first began to wonder about a sibling transference and the role of siblings in our internal world, when I had become stuck for a very long time in a therapy with a female patient, Mrs K. She would repeat an endless litany of her sins and I could make no inroads into her impacted superego. One day she mentioned her elder sister in a way that helped me to grasp that we had been locked into a transference enactment, in which I was this hated sister. It was a striking moment when I took up the sibling transference with her, for it allowed us to unlock a ruthless venom that had been hidden away in one of the harshest superegos I have encountered. For years she had lain on the couch, bottling up her revengeful hatred of me and, instead, had torn herself to shreds. She had experienced me in much the same way as she had experienced her bossy elder sister, and I had not been aware of this possibility (Coles, 1998).

Until that moment, I had never thought about a sibling transference, and I had certainly never read about it. There is no reference to a sibling transference in any of the psychoanalytic dictionaries and Colonna and Newman (1983) are the first writers to draw attention to this fact. The idea that a therapy could become stuck in an undiagnosed sibling transference was not an idea that I had come across.

From the experience with Mrs K, and others, I have come to believe that an extremely harsh superego is often one of the hallmarks of sibling difficulties. Children can be extraordinarily cruel to each other and I hope the following clinical example will give some idea of the relationship of a harsh superego to an experience of sibling cruelty. In the example it will be seen that I worked with a powerful sibling transference for most of the time.

> Mr T, a married man, came into therapy in his late forties. He was the middle child of seven. He had three older sisters and three younger brothers. His parents were tenant farmers and he was brought up in the country. He had been advised to seek psychotherapeutic help by his doctor as he seemed irremediably stressed and depressed. He was on Prozac. I saw him three times a week, but he never lay on the couch. "If I can't see your face, I don't know what you are doing", he remarked when we first met, and he continued to fear me, in this way, throughout the therapy. His fear of me was compounded from many things, but I came to formulate his fears in the following way. The seven children were thrown together to bring each other up, while the parents were engaged in maintaining the rigorous demands of their farm. The consequence was that Mr T's two older sisters were given the task of looking after him. From an early age he remembered being pinched and slapped as they tried to get him dressed in the morning. Meal times were another nightmare, or more accurately, a chaotic free-for-all. When it came to school, again it was his sisters who took him and waited for him at the end. One particularly vivid experience he recounted was walking back from school on a hot summer day. They had a half-mile walk home. He was walking too slowly, his sisters later asserted, and so they ran off without him. He felt lost and completely abandoned, and to this day, the thought of going to a

strange place and not being able to find his way still fills him with a visceral dread.

It can be seen that Mr T's early years came under the powerful influence of his two older sisters, which, in turn, had an effect upon his developing psyche. It was only on rare occasions that he could experience me as a maternal presence that might be available to help him sort through his anxieties. I was even more shadowy as a paternal presence that might be internalized. For the most part, he would come to his sessions, hyperventilating on occasions, in increasing stress. As we tried to unpack the cause of his state of mind, we always got back to his firm conviction that I was one of his sisters, pushing him into the unwelcoming clothes of my psychoanalytic theory and then dismissing him at the end of a session to get lost on his way home. His experience of me was, in some ways, correct, for it was only when I tumbled to the idea that he saw me as one of his older sisters that I realized I had been pushing him into thinking about his difficulties in terms of oedipal and pre-oedipal anxieties. For instance, he suffered extreme anxiety about his sexual fantasies. If they came into his mind he thought that he would be arrested, for he believed they were indelibly written across his brow. In the beginning I tried interpreting his fantasies as expressing oedipal longings to see what I got up to in his absence. When I began to understand that, for the most part, he saw me as one or other of his two older sisters, my understanding of his fantasies changed. He told me that one of the games that his sisters used to play with him was to suddenly pull down his trousers to see if he had an erection. He never knew when they might do this. I could begin to link his terror of his sexually arousing fantasies and this cruel game with his need to keep an eye on me. This led to some important work we did concerning privacy. He needed to find a way in which he could feel that he was able to keep metaphorical hold of his trousers in my presence and not to have to tell me everything that was in his mind. The paradox was that as he felt more able to have a private place for his sexual fantasies, and less obliged to tell me everything, he was able to become more open and feel less vulnerable.

Mr T stayed in therapy for several years and some features of his life changed. He was able to come off Prozac, take early retirement, and develop a passion for cooking. But I was never able to truly assuage the power of Mr T's older sisters in his internal world. They seemed to be "ineradicably fixed" (Freud, 1900a, p. 483) in his unconscious. This has been my experience with other patients with siblings who have been cruel to them.

To give an example, Mr T developed a passion for cooking. I thought that his cooking was a creative way of dealing with the nightmare meals in his childhood. But, I was never able to share usefully with Mr T, that, wonderful though his cooking seemed to be, his insistence that his wife and children sit for two hours over his carefully prepared meals could be seen as exacting some sort of sadistic revenge upon his sisters. I would try and steer my way around this idea, and the moment he sensed I might see something negative in what he was doing, he would be off into a self-flagellating frame of mind, in which he would tell me that the carrots had been overcooked, there was a lump or two in the potato, and he knew he could never roll the pastry out thinly enough. I was never able to soften this tendency in Mr T to lash out at himself when he sensed I was facing him with his own sadism. He would slip into an experience of himself as an outcast on a desert island in a universe of unjust punishment.

I believe there is a relationship between an unjustly harsh superego and the experience of sibling cruelty. The inner fantasies that terrified Mr T, that he would be exposed and abandoned and his sexual desires would be a cause for humiliation, are fantasies that can be found in many different guises in the inner world of us all. The claim that I am making is that I have become alert to the possibility that an obdurate and harsh superego may be linked to the internalization of siblings as figures of authority. This internalization confronts the psyche with difficulties that need to be distinguished from internalized parental figures. For instance, sibling relationships do not seem to be given up or worked through in the way we have come to expect from the oedipal conflict. I was never able to move the sibling transference into a parental oedipal one, for any length of time with Mr T. The reason for this may be linked to the fact that what becomes internalized are the fantasies that the siblings in authority bring to the relationship. In the case of Mr T, his two older sisters seemed to have had little access to more considerate maternal fantasies. Instead they were probably exhausted and frustrated, angry and cruel, and these feelings fed the landscape of Mr T's internalized world of care. In Chapter Five I shall be discussing Klein's view, that the crucial difference between creative sibling relationships and ones that are negative and destructive lie in the nature of the fantasies. Sadistic fantasies that are acted upon between children will be damaging, she suggests.

The experience I have had with Mr T and with Mrs K does not lead me to Freud's belief that siblings seem to be essentially hostile to each other. In these two cases and one or two others (Coles, 1998), their inner world seemed constructed around the warring forces of sibling hostility and the result was a massive distortion of their capacity to love and be loved. However, it does not follow that all sibling relationships are by their nature hostile. I have also experienced a sibling transference that was highly seductive, compelling, and loving (*ibid.*). I will only briefly highlight features of the erotic sibling transference.

Mr Y was the oldest of four children, a younger sister and two younger brothers. Mr Y came from a prosperous middle class family that had known none of the economic hardships that Mr T's family had faced. Mr Y did not have a harsh superego. Nevertheless, he caught me up in a sibling transference that was as powerful as the one with Mr T, though I took time to realize that I had become a much loved, younger sister. In this case I was expected to collude with him in a "secret complicity" (Klein, 1932) against the adults, and indeed I did. I do not mean that I had an affair with him—though I do wonder whether therapies that become sexualized may, in some cases, have foundered on an unrecognized sibling transference—but I was caught up in powerful counter-transference feelings. I would fail to analyse missed sessions when he went off with his girl friend and instead, on one occasion, I overcharged him. I often felt bewildered by what was happening between us, yet he soon became my favourite patient as we seemed to stretch our imagination in sympathetic discourse.

As a young child he and his sister had, one might want to say, fallen in love with each other. I had no reason to believe that it had become a sexualized relationship, but they had become devoted to each other to the exclusion of everyone else. Why had this happened? Were they enacting an oedipal fantasy? Brother and sister against the parents? Their parents were not around much, for they were busy, professional people. All the children had been brought up by a succession of au pair girls and occasional nannies. Mr Y's relationship with his sister came to be the most stable and reliable one that he knew. My experience with Mr Y made me realize that, at the height of the sibling transference, we seemed to be in an exclusive enclave.

This exclusive enclave, that Mr Y and his sister created, grew, I am sure, from a primary desire to be in a dyadic relationship with the maternal object. My argument is that the relationship of loving cooperation that he had with his sister, altered Mr Y's inner world. He drew emotional nurturance and support from her and that gave him an experience that he could not have had with a maternal figure. Therefore, we miss something if we say they were just parenting each other, even though the relationship compensated for parental absences. The lived experience made it different, not least because they were almost the same age. It seemed that their relationship helped to nurture in Mr Y a particular sensibility that determined all his subsequent relationships with women, including his therapist. For instance, there was a subtle way in which he could cooperate or even play with an interpretation that I might make. He could, at times, listen to what I had to say from a place within himself that was untrammelled by what might be called oedipal anxieties, such as the fear of seduction or anxieties about my state of mind. These features were not permanent, of course, but they were moments in which we played together cooperatively, like children, and "child's play" cannot be compared to the games between parents and children. They are different and enrich the psyche in different ways.

These two cases are very extreme. For the most part, my clinical experience suggests that one works with an intermingling and muddle between a sibling transference and a parental one, as in the case of Mrs Z. She was a middle-aged woman married with three children, who came to see me because of panic attacks. As with Mr T, she had an extremely punitive superego, and this alerted me to the possibility of sibling conflicts. I learned that she came from a large family. There were no obvious indications of parental dereliction. In time we came to understand the panic attacks in the following way. Everything that she turned her mind to she needed to do perfectly: perfect mother, perfect patient, perfect secretary, perfect wife. Any lapse from the wished for goal caused an outpouring of self-flagellation which brought on a panic attack. She would panic that she had left a dirty handkerchief in my lavatory, or that she had come to a session at the wrong time, or that she had forgotten to pay me. All of these were run-of-the-mill anxieties about her fear of her negative feelings. But Mrs Z seemed to need to cling to her self-image. I had, by now, become more confident that I could sense the differences between a sibling transference and a parental transference, and the way both could duck in and out of a session. I was able to sense that there were times when her anxiety that she had not paid me could be associated to a fiercely competitive sibling transference in which she wished to be the one receiving the money, not me. At other times the anxiety was more to do with her aggressive fantasies towards me as a maternal figure, with too many babies, and not enough time for her. It was Mrs Z who was able to tell me that she realized she was strung between two incompatible claims. On the one hand, she wanted to have all the attention and the limelight. She wanted her parents' assurance that they preferred her to her siblings and that they thought her the most beautiful and intelligent. However, the moment that she felt close to achieving some recognition for herself, she knew that it would put her relationship with her siblings into jeopardy. She knew she needed them. She did not know how to straddle the conflict between the wish to be the preferred child and the wish to be part of the sibling clan. I felt that Mrs Z's incompatible wishes were very real.

One way of conceptualizing Mrs Z's difficulty might be in terms of Sharpe and Rosenblatt's (1994) *Oedipal Sibling Triangles*. They take the view that sibling relationships are "engendered autonomously" (p. 494), and that these relationships develop structurally through a pre-oedipal and dyadic phase to an oedipal triadic phase. In families where there are several siblings, the children will create triangles among themselves that are independent of oedipal parental triangles and these triangles exert a powerful influence upon psychic development. These oedipal sibling triangles can involve two children and one parent or three children. They are not the same as the original oedipal triangle of parents and one child, but they "are sufficiently similar to the standard oedipal triad in dynamics and structural elements" (p. 492).

Sharpe and Rosenblatt (1994) endorse my view that there will be certain characteristics of a sibling transference that will help to distinguish it from a parental one. "A big brother transference will usually entail attitudes of mingled admiration and more openly intense competition" (p. 493). In contrast, a paternal transference, "will usually embody a more ambivalent submission and rebellion" (*ibid.*). The difficulty of distinguishing between these two ways of relating is that a patient can move very rapidly between them within a session, as I discovered with Mrs Z. For instance, there could be exciting moments with Mrs Z, when I would feel that we had understood something, or made some "progress", only to discover that this "excitement" involved a "secret complicity" (Klein, 1932) against some authority figure. The excitement could be quickly negated into a sullen rebellion if I was heavy handed with my response.

Some oedipal-like triangles among siblings may be a displacement from parental oedipal issues, as in the case of Mr Y and his sister. It could be said that they were playing "mothers and fathers" against the adult world of absent parents and au pair girls. But as I have already said, the repercussions upon the psyche of taking a sibling as love object alters the inner world in a radical way, and I agree with Sharpe and Rosenblatt (1994) that it "seems to reflect an error common in the psychoanalytic literature" that these subtle dynamics do not become distinguished.

In families where there are several children, sibling oedipal conflict is not only different from parental oedipal conflict, but its resolution is different, and in many cases, more difficult. In particular, the most difficult cases are those that are constellated between two siblings and a parent, and in which it is the parent who is the oedipal rival to the siblings' relationship. I think this is an important area that needs further exploration and clinical support. In my experience with Mr Y, though it seemed that his mother and caretakers were happy to let the children create a magical world together, it became clear, through my counter-transference enactment when I overcharged him, that I was acting out the role of the jealous mother in rivalry with his girlfriend/sister. I believe that this maternal jealousy helped to reinforce the strength of the sibling tie.

Sharpe and Rosenblatt (1994) refer to another intractable "oedipal sibling triangle" that occurs between two siblings who are in rivalry over a third sibling. In their view, there are several important elements in this constellation that make it more intense than parental oedipal triangles. A child engaged in parental oedipal struggles has two conflicting claims, to be the sole possessor of one parent and at the same time the wish to be loved and taken care of by both parents. With siblings, the dynamics are different. Siblings have easier access to acting out their wishes and desires, whether hostile or loving, and this results in a greater intensity of feeling, which in turn becomes less easy to relinquish. Not only is there less need or desire to overcome oedipal sibling triangles, but the narcissistic blow to the self-esteem that results from the loss of the battle means that there is far greater investment in continuing the battle rather than giving it up, in contrast to parent and child oedipal conflict.

Sharpe and Rosenblatt (1994) illustrate this with the example of a man, Jake, who came from a family of six boys. Jake had become the most successful of the brothers but "he felt anguished and hollow about this victory" (p. 503). One reason for his anguish was that he had competed with his older brother Frank not only for his father's attention, but also for that of a younger brother, Tommy, to whom Frank was very close. This "sibling triangle" eventually resulted in Jake, Frank, and Tommy all engaging simultaneously in homo-sexual activity, with Jake vying with Tommy for Frank's attention. Jake soon withdrew from the *ménage à trois*, but continued to "exploit and verbally abuse Tommy" (*ibid.*). When later Tommy became "a wasted drug addict" (*ibid.*), Jake was overwhelmed by guilt. His guilt was more intense and difficult to overcome than his oedipal difficulties with his father.

I discovered Sharpe and Rosenblatt's work subsequent to therapy with Mr T and Mr Y so I did not pursue with them the idea that they might have been caught up in "oedipal sibling triangles". I was aware that Mr T seemed stuck in a lonely world of siblings with little recourse to parental help, rather as Tommy in the case above. And in the case of Mr Y, it could be said that he and his sister had created an "oedipal sibling triangle" against the adults and their other siblings. Mrs Z's anguish, between the wish to be the favoured child of her parents and to be one of the sibling gang, could also be explained as a conflict between two competing oedipal triangles, a parental one and a sibling one.

How can we pick out strong sibling attachments? Are there any fantasies that might be associated with a sibling identification? I have suggested that an extremely harsh superego alerts me to possible sibling conflicts. In such cases, there seems to be an inability to face and deal with their own sadism and cruelty. They live in a world where the chief experience is of martyrdom and masochism. If they are hurt by others, they believe they deserve it. They imagine the solution to their pain is to struggle, yet again, to be perfect. A typical fantasy may be, as with Mr T, that he could create a perfect meal, and when he met any conflict or criticism, he did not have recourse to a soothing internal figure who could love and appreciate his struggle and his creativity. This, as I understand it, is because a cruel sibling has been internalized, who does not have the nurturing capacities that a parental figure more usually possesses. This was the figure I represented for Mr T, and I did little to shift such a firmly held belief.

In the case of Mr Y, who had internalized a sibling with whom there had been a more loving and cooperative experience, there was a fantasy of a "secret complicity" (Klein, 1932) against the adults, an "us" against "them". In the transference, I became caught up in a counter-transference enactment with him which had all the hall-marks of such a fantasy. In Chapter Five I shall look in detail at Klein's theory on the importance of sibling love and attachment, for as I will argue throughout this book, I believe Klein is making an important claim when she suggests that the "secret complicity" of incestuous desire between siblings, "plays an essential part in every relationship of love, even, between grown-up people" (1932, p. 224). Such an idea presents us with a psychoanalytic theory of mind which challenges the idea that sexual development only involves the resolution of oedipal conflict. The nature of sibling sexual desire and its impact on adult sexual relationships, is still an uncharted area that needs careful exploration, and we may well find that the capacity to experience sibling desire enriches our capacity for mature sexual fulfilment.

In this chapter I have been suggesting that sibling relationships and therefore a sibling transference, can play a crucial part in understanding unconscious conflicts. I have also been suggesting that sibling relationships are "engendered autonomously" (Sharpe & Rosenblatt, 1994), and that we miss the richness of the inner world if we see them as "second editions" (Colonna & Newman, 1983) of the parental triad. In the following chapters I shall be following the question as to why we have neglected siblings in our analytic theories. Has psychoanalytic theory, in ignoring the place siblings have in the psyche, enacted the fantasy of the jealous sibling, who hopes that if he or she ignores the other siblings they will go away?

CHAPTER TWO

Freud and siblings

"As a rule there is only one person an English girl hates more than she hates her eldest sister; and that's her mother"

Shaw, 1948

"As a rule there is only one person an English girl hates more than she hates her mother; and that's her elder sister"

Freud, 1916–1917, p. 205

F reud's misquotation from Shaw, was highlighted by Penelope Farmer (2000) in her anthology on sisters, and it serves as a nice illustration of Freud's "Freudian slip" (p. 190) in his thinking about siblings. He did not much care for them, his own or those of anyone else, and there are only passing references to them in his theoretical work, (1900a, 1905d, 1910a, 1914f, 1916–1917, 1931b), and no reference to them in his intellectual autobiography (1935a) despite the fact that he had five sisters and one brother. One result of Freud's comparative neglect of the place of siblings in emotional development, has been that there is almost no mention of siblings in psychoanalytic theory or practice and it is assumed that siblings play little part in people's health or mental distress, with the exception of Mitchell (2000).

The place that siblings have in Freud's work is as competitors for parental attention. He has been credited, quite rightly, with having normalized sibling rivalry.

> The elder child ill-treats the younger, maligns him and robs him of his toys; while the younger is consumed with impotent rage against the elder, envies and fears him. [Freud, 1900a, p 250]

There is little genuine love between siblings, and cooperative behaviour is always a form of expediency. "If one cannot be the favourite oneself, at all events nobody else shall be favourite." In this way jealousy is replaced by "group feelings". (Freud, 1921c, p. 120).

Freud's view, that the essential nature of sibling relationships is one of jealousy, is supported by the Judaeo–Christian culture of the Old Testament, which is redolent with sibling murder and rivalry. The tales of Cain and Abel, Jacob and Esau, and Joseph and his brothers are much quoted examples. What Freud ignored in his theoretical writing, as Raphael-Leff (1990) has pointed out, were the more complicated tales of sibling love and hate that can be found in Egyptian mythology. It would be unfair to accuse Freud of ignoring Egyptian mythology if he had never shown any interest in their culture, but his consulting room contained more Egyptian than Greek figures (Raphael-Leff, 1990) and he was equally enthralled by both cultures. Why then did he take the myth of Oedipus as the metaphor of human psychic development? Does it provide the best model of unconscious generational sexual conflict?

There are other myths, that Freud knew, which contain much fuller accounts of the unconscious dynamics of sexual conflicts within the family. An important example is the myth of Isis and Osiris in which parents and children are not the only people in this drama, but the passions of sibling rivalry and murder, as well as sibling love and cooperation, are given equal prominence. This myth takes a more sanguine view about sibling incest, a point that I shall develop in Chapter Six, and this is in marked contrast to the Greek myth of Oedipus, in which the breaking of the incest taboo brings everyone to a tragic end.

The myth goes as follows. Isis and Osiris were brother and sister, as well as King and Queen of Egypt. Their parents Geb, the God of Earth, and Nut, Goddess of the Sky, were also brother and sister. Isis and Osiris had siblings, Seth and Nephthys, who were also married to each other. It was said that Osiris, as King of Egypt, brought great peace and prosperity to his people. However, his brother Seth was jealous of him. One day Seth invited his brother to a feast and presented him with a chest. He asked Osiris to get into the chest, which Osiris did, and the chest was thrown into the Nile. Osiris was drowned, dismembered, and scattered over the world by Seth. Isis, Osiris' wife, was heart-broken. She searched the world for his remains, and found them all, save his phallus. She put him together, with help from her sister Nephthys, and, by using a wooden phallus, she was able to conceive a son, Horus. She had to hide herself and Horus from Seth, who wanted to kill them. Meanwhile, Osiris languished, emasculated, in the underworld. Horus grew to manhood and, when he had acquired sufficient skill and strength, he fought with Seth. Seth ripped out Horus' left eye and Horus tore off Seth's testicles. Finally, Horus was declared King of Egypt and Seth was punished for the murder of his brother by being turned into a boat that had to carry Osiris forever. Horus descended into the underworld to look for his father, Osiris. When he found him they embraced and exchanged *ka* (said to be male generative power). Horus gave Osiris his left eye, torn out by Seth and, as a result, Osiris was regenerated and able to reign in the Underworld. Horus returned to Earth and became a Pharaoh (Raphael-Leff, 1990; Whitehead, 1986).

The point of recounting this myth, in such detail, is to draw attention to the richness and complexity of the drama. There is sibling incest, sibling jealousy, and murder, but there is also sibling and parental love and cooperation and all these emotions are held in equal balance. Or, to put it another way, each of the emotions that are expressed have equal claim to be considered in their own right, rather than one emotion being prioritized over any other.

I am now going to turn to the Oedipus myth in order to compare it with the Isis and Osiris myth. In Graves (1955), Laius, son of Labdacus, is banished from Thebes and visits King Pelops. Laius falls in love with Pelops illegitimate son, Chrissippus. When Laius is allowed to return to Thebes he takes Chrissippus with him as his lover. Chrissippus dies and Laius is accused of his murder. When

Laius marries Jocasta they are childless. Laius consults the oracle and is told that if he were to have a child it would murder him. In response to the oracle Laius refuses to make love to Jocasta, but does not tell her why. One night Jocasta gets Laius drunk and seduces him. Nine months later a son, Oedipus, is born and Laius takes the child away. The child's feet are pierced with a nail, bound together, and he is put on Mount Cithaeron to die. He is rescued and brought up by the King and Queen of Corinth as their own child. As a young man, Oedipus is teased because he does not look like his parents, so he goes to the Delphic Oracle and is told that he will kill his father and marry his mother.

He decides he must leave Corinth forever to avoid his fate, but, on the road from Delphi, he meets Laius, who is on his way to consult the Oracle as to how to get rid of the Sphinx that was harassing the Thebans—Laius had brought this blight upon the Thebans by enraging the goddess Hera for abducting the boy Chrissippus. Father and son meet at a crossroad with fatal results. Laius orders Oedipus to get out of his way. Oedipus is enraged and kills Laius' charioteer and this results in Laius being dragged to his death by the chariot. Oedipus goes on to Thebes and is able to answer the Sphinx's riddle and the Sphinx hurls herself to her death. Oedipus is declared the new king of Thebes. He marries Jocasta, unaware that she is his mother, and has four children. A plague ravages Thebes and so Oedipus consults the Oracle again and he is told that the murderer of Laius has to be exiled. Oedipus is eventually told, by blind Tiresias, that he was the murderer of Laius. Jocasta kills herself and Oedipus blinds himself with a pin taken from her garment. He exiles himself from Thebes and is accompanied by his daughter Antigone. He dies at Colonus and is buried in Athens.

It can be seen from this account that the Oedipus myth carries the weight of homosexuality and murder, deception and abandonment. Freud has two interpretations. In 1900a, he tells the tale in much the same way as Graves, and suggests that what moves us about Sophocles' tragedy is that it stirs up in us universal infantile sexual wishes and conflict. In 1912–1913, Freud suggests that this universal conflict has a phylogenetic history, in which paternal violence plays an important part in the drama.

In Freud's earliest account of the Oedipus myth, the comparison to the Isis and Osiris myth is striking. Oedipus is alone in a universe that has been hostile from the moment of his conception. There is little idea of cooperation, companionship or creative restoration to set against the backdrop of the violence that has been done to him. He has been mutilated and rejected by his parents, and manages to survive in a world of half-truths. When the truth is known he is blinded by it and exiled.

Does the myth embody a universal psychic truth? Some authors have been of the opinion that Freud had a "tendency to emphasize the aggressive elements of intergenerational dynamics over the mutually affirmative themes which dominate the Egyptian mytho-poetic creation" (Whitehead, 1986, p. 77). Others have pointed out that Oedipus' fate was determined, not so much by his own wishes, as by the cruel actions of his parents.

> Laius tried to kill Oedipus—and with mother Jocasta's help. The infant with the pierced feet hung from the tree to perish ... This picture has to be montaged with the image of the patricide and of cohabiting with his mother. [Schlesinger, 1969, p. 60]

In Freud's later view, that the Oedipus myth is the result or consequence of the phylogenetic history of parental violence, Oedipus' conflictual and murderous sexual fantasies are slightly shifted. They are precipitated by the cruelty and abandonment of his parents. This idea is developed in the work of Laplanche (1989, 1999) and others. Prierl (2002) suggested that the: "traditional psychoanalytic reading of Oedipus emerge[s] from an individualistic concept of the human subject", and fails to take account of "Merope's and Polybus's silence and of Laius's and Jocasta's transgressions and violence, centring on the unconscious messages proffered by others" (p. 441).

The Oedipus myth has held great significance in Western culture, because it emphasizes a tragic aspect of human experience. The Horus–Osiris myth directs our attention to the possibility that though murder and jealousy, incestuous desire and sibling rivalry may be rife within the psyche, there are other fundamental elements of love and cooperation to be found as well. At the very least, the myth of Isis and Osiris suggests that sibling relationships are much richer and more varied than Freud suggested.

We seem to have no difficulty in accepting Freud's belief in sibling rivalry. The more difficult question is whether siblings can love each other. The way Freud formulates sibling relationships suggests that sibling love and cooperation are always a form of expediency, and such a view leads to scepticism about a deeply held cultural belief in brotherly love.

I believe siblings can genuinely love each other, and the games they create amongst themselves may be some of the most precious moments of a remembered childhood. George Eliot was aware of the intensity of sibling passion, and the difficulty we all have in recognizing it. Her early novel, *The Mill on the Floss* (1860), has as its dominant theme, the relationship between a brother, Tom, and his younger sister, Maggie. We follow the vicissitudes of their relationship as they grow up and face adult sexuality. Perhaps it would be an exaggeration to say that *The Mill on the Floss* is a morality tale about the failure to recognize the significance of sibling love and attachment. However, it would be true to say that Tom's recognition of his love for Maggie and his realization of her love for him come too late to save them from drowning.

> It was not until Tom had pushed off and they were on the wide water—he face to face with Maggie—that the full meaning of what had happened rushed upon his mind. It came with so overpowering a force—it was such a new revelation to his spirit, of the depths in life that had lain beyond his vision, which he had fancied so keen and clear—that he was unable to ask a question. [1992, p. 596]

Even though Tom is "unable to ask a question", the reader is left in no doubt that this "new revelation to his spirit" is about his recognition of their love for each other and we are reconciled to their death as we remember "the days when they had clasped their little hands in love, and roamed the daisied fields together" (p. 597).

In this novel, George Eliot is able to describe what it feels like to be the eldest sibling as well the emotions of the younger one. She has Maggie assert:

> I love Tom so dearly ... better than anybody else in the world. When he grows up, I shall keep his house, and we shall always live together. I can tell him everything he doesn't know. But I think Tom's clever, for he doesn't like books; he makes beautiful whipcord and rabbit-pens. [*ibid.*, p. 31]

George Eliot also intuitively knew that the emotions older siblings have for younger ones are more complicated by jealousy and rivalry, whereas the struggle of the younger one is to accommodate this hostility and still find a way to be loved and accepted. For instance, Tom buys Maggie a fishing line so that they can go fishing together, for he assumes that Maggie will do what he wants. In other words, Tom has more difficulty in thinking about Maggie's point of view. Maggie, in turn, is happy to fit into this assumption. Or again, Tom asserts, "I don't love you" (p. 38), when he discovers that Maggie has failed to feed his rabbits and they have consequently died, whereas she laments, "Oh, Tom, ... I'd forgive you, if *you* forgot anything—I wouldn't mind what you did—I'd forgive you and love you" (*ibid.*). Maggie's love and hate for Tom is not identical with Tom's love and hate for her. In this novel George Eliot exquisitely delineates the complexity of emotions between siblings, but we do not question the emotional importance they have for each other.

Harriet Martineau, in 1877, writing about her childhood with several older brothers and one older sister, decided that when her younger sister was born, "I would look for my happiness to the new little sister, and that she would never want for the tenderness which I had never found" (Martineau, 1877, p. 51). She was making a decision that was connected to being a child amongst many, a child who felt unloved by her parents and misunderstood by her older siblings. She needed someone to love and happily there was a younger sister who became the object of that love.

Why did Freud neglect the positive aspects of sibling relationships and exclude them from playing any part in the internal world? Freud, like George Eliot, had an intuitive appreciation of the emotional impact of sibling relationships, and yet his theoretical beliefs led him to reject the idea that sibling relationships could form a part of the structure of the psyche. In a letter to Fliess on the 3rd October 1897 (Masson, 1985) and again in his *Interpretation of Dreams* (1900a), he described the quasi-sibling relationship he had with his nephew, John, who was one year older than Freud, and with whom he grew up during the first three years of his life.

> Until the end of my third year we had been inseparable; we had loved each other and fought each other, and ... this childhood

relationship ... had a determining influence on all my subsequent relations with contemporaries. Since that time my nephew John had had many re-incarnations which revived now one side and now another of his personality, unalterably fixed as it was in my unconscious memory ... All my friends have in a certain sense been re-incarnations of the first figure ... They have been "revenants"... My emotional life has always insisted that I should have an intimate friend and a hated enemy. I have always been able to provide myself afresh with both, and it has not infrequently happened that the ideal situation of childhood has been so completely reproduced that friend and enemy have come together in a single individual. [1900a, pp. 424 & 483]

Freud is stating here that his relationship with his nephew John determined all his relationships with his contemporaries. I do not believe Freud felt that this relationship was a "reaction formation" or that John was "a substitute for his faithless mother". Freud is describing a relationship that, for him, stood separate from his relationship with his parents and, by implication, he is suggesting that mature relationships with contemporaries may have their seeds in peer group/sibling experience. However, nowhere in Freud's writing on the structure of the psyche do we find such an insight incorporated into his theory.

In his famous case studies of Dora (1905e), Little Hans (1909b), and "The Wolfman" (1918b), Freud is tender and sympathetic to the fact that siblings do engage with each other when young. In Dora (1905e), he says:

Dora herself had a clear picture of a scene from her early childhood in which she was sitting on the floor in a corner sucking her left thumb and at the same time tugging with her right hand at the lobe of her brother's ear as he sat quietly beside her. [p. 51]

Yet Freud neglects those moments when it comes to understanding Dora's later encounters with men. Why does he take the fact that Dora and her brother had grown more distant from each other in adolescence, to mean that their earlier relationship was without psychic effect? He seems to assume that because, "... in the last few years the relations between the brother and sister had grown more distant" (p. 21), their relationship could have no impact upon her adult wishes and difficulties. I believe that one reason for his failure to find a theoretical way to accommodate the impact of sibling relationships is that he was beginning to formulate his oedipal theory as central to emotional development and neurosis. It followed from that thought that Dora's mental state must be the result of her jealousy of her father's relationship with Frau K and her wish that Herr K might "triumph ... over all her internal difficulties" (p. 109). The emotional impact of sibling attachments confuses the clear trajectory of oedipal desire. Freud takes up a similar position with the Wolfman (1918b), as I shall argue in the next chapter, and as a result, ignores the significance of the sibling relationship.

Freud's theoretical belief about the hostile nature of sibling attachment is in conflict with his intuitive sense that sibling/peer relationships can determine the way we relate to our contemporaries, as he claimed about his relationship with John. This difficulty is further compounded by Freud's anthropological theory on siblings. He thought that the fear of incest, and the elaborate social systems to prevent it, underlie not only parental relationships, but sibling relationships as well (1900a, 1909d, 1912–1913, 1916–1917, 1918b).

> ... an inexorable prohibition ... would not be needed if there were any reliable natural barriers against the temptation to incest. The truth is just opposite. A human being's first choice of an object is regularly an incestuous one, aimed, in the case of the male, at his mother and sister; and it calls for the severest prohibitions to deter this persistent infantile tendency from realization. [1916–1917, p. 335]

Or, put more firmly three years earlier:

> Psychoanalysis has taught us that a boy's earliest choice of objects for his love is incestuous and that those objects are forbidden ones— his mother and his sister. [1912–1913, p. 17]

In other words, Freud believed brothers and sisters have a strong incestuous attraction and they, as well as parents, can have a claim to be early love objects. If that is the case, then where are these sibling incestuous attachments in Freud's case histories?

It seems that Freud's anthropological belief, that siblings can have incestuous desires for each other and be each other's first love object, is in conflict with his psychological belief in the primacy of infantile sexual desire for the parents. He considered that, at the beginning of infant life, it does not matter to whom the infant is attached, as long as the infant's basic needs are being met.

> The child's first choice of an object, which derives from its need for help, claims our further interest. Its choice is directed in the first instance to all those who look after it, but these *soon* give place to its parents. [1910a, p. 47, my emphasis]

This is an extremely important point. He seems to be saying that whatever the earliest experience of attachment might have been, it will be replaced by attachment to parents from whom all significant emotional experience is derived. In other words, even if "the child's first choice of an object" is not a parent, this early attachment will "soon" be given up in the oedipal phase and our emotional desires will become centred upon our parents.

The work of Bowlby (1980) and other attachment theorists, such as S. A. Mitchell (1988) and Holmes (1993), have given us strong arguments to show that the earliest attachments we make leave a lasting imprint upon the psyche. I think that one of the reasons that siblings get left out of Freud's theory is that he glosses over the psychic implications of "the child's first choice of an object". I believe that in the internal world, if your sister is your "first choice of an object", you will find her there and she will be different from a mother, father or Nanya (see Chapter Four on "The Wolfman"). Even if your sister is "a substitute for your faithless mother", (1916–1917, p. 334), the emotional contours of this relationship will be substantially different from the one you would have had if she had been your mother, whatever her age. I illustrated this difference in Chapter One when I took up the concept of a sibling transference in clinical work. Brothers and sisters tend to be of the same generation, and if they have been each other's "first choice of object" we can safely assume that they will not have the same conscious or unconscious concerns as parents. Why do we need to dismiss this difference? What would be lost?

The reason for Freud's belief that the earliest attachments can be replaced by parental attachments is, as I have already suggested, to do with the importance he placed upon his emerging theory of the Oedipus complex. If the wish to marry your mother and kill your father are the essential unconscious wishes of the psyche, and from these wishes the structure of the psyche is determined, then it follows that an attachment to a sibling must be no more than a parental substitute. However, I believe there was another reason why Freud turned his back on the importance of sibling attachments. This reason was linked to the complexity of relationships in his own family of origin. Freud had emotional, as well as intellectual, reasons for believing that siblings, and also nannies, do not affect our psychic development. In the next chapter I shall turn to the early years of Freud's own life to try to understand something of these emotional reasons.

CHAPTER THREE

Freud's early years

F reud's father Jakob was forty when, in 1855, he married Freud's mother, Amalia Nathansohn, who was only twenty. Jakob brought with him two sons, Emanuel and Philipp, from an earlier marriage. Emanuel, in his early twenties, was himself married with a son, John, this same John who became Freud's "inseparable companion" (Freud, 1900a). Philipp would have been nineteen or twenty-one (Jones, 1953; Raphael-Leff, 1990). Emanuel and Philipp probably lived next door to Jakob and Amalia. Indeed "the half-brother Emanuel's family lived so near and was so intimate that the two families might be regarded as one" (Jones, 1953, p. 6).

In May 1856 Freud was born. His grandfather, Jakob's father, had just died, (Raphael-Leff, 1990, p. 324), and his parents were squashed into "a single rented room in a modest house ... (in) Freiberg" (Gay, 1988, p. 7). The circumstances surrounding Freud's early years were to prove most complicated and quite unpropitious. It is not clear, from either Jones or Gay, whether the family continued to live in this "single rented room" until they left Freiberg in 1859, but equally there is no evidence that they moved before leaving Freiberg (Anzieu, 1986). It is my suspicion, as I shall argue in the next chapter, that indeed they did remain in that one room for the first three years of Freud's life, and that this experience was fundamental to Freud's analytic theories, as well as his treatment of the Wolfman.

In spite of their poverty and the death of Jakob's father, his family turned Freud's birth into something noteworthy. He had been born in a caul and this was said to be " . . . an event which was believed to ensure him future happiness" (Jones, 1953, p. 5). Freud (1916–1917) also came to believe that he was his mother's "undisputed darling", even though he could also assert that there was "nothing worth remembering" of the "long and difficult years" of this early period (1899a, p. 312).

In 1857, the year following Freud's birth, his brother Julius was born and died a few months later. Gay (1988) says that there is "contentious scholarship" (p. 656) surrounding Freud's early life, and it is not known whether Freud's mother was already pregnant again when Julius died, or whether Freud's sister, Anna, born in December 1858, was a "replacement baby" (Raphael-Leff, 1990, p. 325). Nor can we be sure whether Freud's mother lost her own brother, Julius, just before or just after the birth of her son Julius. (Estelle Roith suggested that it was more likely that Julius, following a Jewish tradition, was named after his dead grandfather. *Personal communication.*) We do know that Amalia's brother, Julius, died in March 1858 (Raphael-Leff, 1990, p. 324). What we can say with absolute certainty was that during these "long and difficult years" the young Freud was in the midst of a 'bewildering texture of familial relationships" (Gay, 1988, p. 5), and, we need to add, "a bewildering texture" of family losses.

Freud's family left Freiberg in 1859 and further losses ensued. Freud lost three close relatives; his "inseparable companion" (Freud, 1900a), John, John's sister, Pauline, whom Freud remembers treating cruelly (Masson, 1985, p. 268) and John's father Emmanuel, who was Freud's half-brother. As has already been said, the two families had intermingled as one large family during these early years, but when the Freud household left Freiberg, Emmanuel and his family moved to England and Freud scarcely saw them again. At one blow, Freud lost his home, and "the beautiful woods near our home" (1899a, p. 312), and his extended family. But Freud had also suffered another earlier loss.

When he was two-and-a-half years old his nurse, Monika Zadjic (Anzieu, 1986), who had looked after him since birth, was suddenly dismissed. She was found to have stolen some of Freud's toys and money. This incident coincided with Amalia's absence during the birth of Freud's sister, Anna (Gay, 1990; Jones, 1953). It is not hard to imagine the drama that this must have caused in the Freud household. Amalia was preoccupied with Anna, and Jakob may have been away, for he spent six months of the year travelling (Ellenberger, 1970). Freud's half-brother, Philipp, seems to have been in charge of the household at this time, for it was he who fired Monika Zadjic and oversaw her imprisonment. Who was attending to Freud? Freud, in later life, referred to his nurse as "the prehistoric old woman" (1900a, p. 248). Nevertheless, she was clearly an important figure, for he said: "It was reasonable to suppose that the child loved the old woman who taught him these lessons (of cleanliness), in spite of her rough treatment of him" (*ibid.*).

The reason for elaborating on these early years in Freud's life is because I am suggesting it was from the matrix of these losses that his psychological theories were woven. I wish to show that the effect of the loss of his brother, Julius, the loss of his Nurse, the loss of his mother during the birth of Anna, may help to explain why siblings have a marginal place in the way in which he conceived of emotional development.

The loss of his brother, Julius, when Freud was under two, was perhaps the most traumatic event that he suffered during his first three years. When he was sixty he seemed to be looking back upon this difficult and confusing time. He wrote:

When other children appear on the scene the Oedipus complex is enlarged into a family complex. This, with fresh support from the egoistic sense of injury, gives grounds for receiving the new brothers or sisters with repugnance and for unhesitatingly getting rid of them by a wish. It is even true that as a rule children are far readier to give verbal expression to *these* feelings of hate than to those arising from the parental complex. If a wish of this kind is fulfilled and the undesired addition to the family is removed again shortly afterwards by death, we can discover from a later analysis what an important experience this death has been to the child. [1916–1917, pp. 333–334]

However he stops there. He does not go on, as we might expect, and tell us what the effect of this death might have been upon the child who survives. Instead he swiftly turns away and in the next sentence he says:

> A child who has been put into second place by the birth of a brother or sister, and who is now for the first time almost isolated from his mother, does not easily forgive her this loss of place; feelings which in an adult would be described as greatly embittered arise in him and are often the basis of a permanent estrangement. [*ibid.*]

Raphael-Leff (1990) has suggested: "... the death of this baby (Julius) was probably the most significant emotional event in Freud's entire life and remained encapsulated as an unprocessed wordless area of prehistoric deathly rivalry and identification" (p. 325). The idea that Freud was never able to come to terms with the death of his brother, Julius, seems to be confirmed in his original records on the "Rat-Man" (1909d).

> Oct. 12. ... I have not mentioned from earlier sessions three interrelated memories dating from his (The Ratman's) fourth year, which he describes as his earliest ones and which refer to the death of his elder sister Katherine. The first was of her being carried to bed. The second was of his asking "Where is Katherine?" and going into the room and finding his father sitting in an arm-chair weeping. The third was of his father bending over his weeping mother. [p. 264]

On October 14th, Freud notes:

> My uncertainty and forgetfulness on these last two points seem to be intimately connected. The memories were really his and the consideration which I had forgotten was that once he was very young and he and his sister were talking about death, she said: "On my soul, if you die I shall kill myself". So that in both cases it was a question of his sister's death. (*They were forgotten owing to complexes of my own.*). [*ibid.*, p. 264, italics mine]

Mitchell (2000) extends the idea of the effect of Freud's dead brother onto the development of psychoanalysis: "This unacknowledged dead brother can be said to have 'possessed' the theory of psychoanalysis, ever present in the accounts but completely unintegrated into the theory or practice" (p. 239) and it would certainly help us to understand why Freud necessarily made no reference to his dead sibling in the quotation above. But I want to suggest that, before we can fully account for the more general marginalization of siblings in Freud's thinking, we have to look at the way in which he marginalized the "prehistoric old woman", his nurse.

In the early years of Freud's exploration of the unconscious, he was troubled by the accounts of his patient's tales of seduction. At the same time, through his own self-analysis, he was discovering troubling thoughts about his own father. On 8th February 1897 he wrote to Fliess, "Unfortunately, my own father was one of these perverts and is responsible for the hysteria of my brother ... and those of several younger sisters" (Masson, 1985, pp. 230–231). A few months later, on the 21st of September 1897, he wrote to Fliess: "I no longer believe in my *neurotica*" (p. 265).[1] This was followed a few days later, on 3rd October, by a lengthy explanation:

> I can only indicate that the old man [Freud's father] plays no active part in my case, but that no doubt I drew an inference by analogy from myself onto him; that in my case the "prime originator" was an ugly, elderly, but clever woman [Freud's nurse]. [*ibid.*, pp. 268– 269]

Finally, as a footnote to this letter, on the 4th of October, he writes:

> Today's dream has, under the strangest disguises, produced the following: she was my teacher in sexual matters and complained because I was clumsy and unable to do anything ... Moreover, she washed me in reddish water in which she had previously washed herself. [*ibid.*]

How should we understand his dream that "revealed" that his nurse had been his "teacher in sexual matters, ... (who) complained because I was clumsy and unable to do anything"? His concept of a "screen memory" had not yet been formulated. Was this a memory of what today would be called sexual abuse? It does not seem that Freud was unduly dismayed by this self-revelation for, on October 15th, he wrote to Fliess: "A single idea of general value dawned on me. I have found, in my own case too, [the phenomenon of] being in love with my mother and jealous of my father, and now consider it a universal event in early childhood" (*ibid.*, p. 272). He no longer believed that his own hysteria, or that of his brother and sisters, was the result of their father's perverse behaviour. He replaced this belief with an idea that is strangely ambiguous in its meaning. He exempted his father from all culpability, because he realized that it had been his nurse who had initiated him into sexual matters. However, it is left there, and no more is said, and an uneasy and confusing moment with his nurse becomes subsumed under a universal myth about parents. He seems to have turned his back on nurses and looked towards the real parents, and in so doing, siblings are also withdrawn from having a central part in the unfolding drama of psychic development.

I am suggesting that there is a note of relief in his letter to Fliess of the 15th of October, 1897. "A single idea of general value dawned on me ... a universal event in early childhood." Freud's nurse may have been "his first choice of object", she may even have seduced him, but ultimately she was not significant in her own right, he seems to be saying. He found that his parents were all that mattered. The beauty of the oedipal theory is that it simplifies early attachment to nannies and to siblings and to the generational mix-up of attachments in Freud's family. Gay (1988) is surely right when he suggests that Freud's mind was made up of "childhood conundrums" (p. 6) in which his half-brother was a father, his father was a grandfather to his closest playmate, he himself was an uncle to his older nephew, his mother was the same age as his half-brother and his "rival", Julius, had been removed by a wish. It was from this generational mix-up that he would weave the "the fabric of his psychoanalytic theories". (*ibid.*). Brilliant though Freud's insight was into the importance of the Oedipus complex, it has had the consequence of marginalizing sibling attachment and reducing siblings to substitute figures in the oedipal drama.

Note

1. Freud's *neurotica* was his belief that "in all cases, the *father*, not excluding my own, had to be accused of being perverse". He gave Fliess several reasons why he no longer believed this to be true.

    (i) "The continual disappointment in my efforts to bring a single analysis to a real conclusion."

(ii) "The realisation of the unexpected frequency of hysteria, with precisely the same conditions prevailing in each."

(iii) "The [incidence] of perversion would have to be immeasurably more frequent."

(iv) "There are no indications of reality in the unconscious."

(v) "The unconscious memory does not break through" (Masson, 1985, pp. 264–265).

CHAPTER FOUR

"The Wolfman"

I ended the last chapter by suggesting that Freud's neglect of the role of siblings in emotional development might be linked to the centrality he gives to the Oedipus complex. In this chapter, I shall be considering what Freud was to call, "a modification of the Oedipus complex" (1939a, p. 79), that is to say the central importance Freud gives to the trauma of seeing and hearing the primal scene. I think we see the result of Freud's belief in the trauma of witnessing the primal scene, in the way he treated "The Wolfman" (1918b). More importantly, for my argument, the consequence of this belief pushes the effect of sibling relationships to the periphery of the psyche.

"The Wolfman" went into analysis with Freud in 1910, when he was twenty-four, following a long period in a German sanatorium where he had been diagnosed as suffering from "manic depressive insanity" (1918b, p. 8). Freud asserts that this depression had been brought on as a consequence of a gonorrhoeal infection when he was eighteen. At the age of eighty-three, "The Wolfman" gave a different account in his *Recollections of My Childhood* (1973). He believed that it was the suicide of his sister Anna, four years earlier in 1906, that had precipitated his depression.

After the death of Anna, with whom I had had a very deep, personal, inner relationship, and whom I had always considered as my only comrade, I fell into a state of deepest depression. [*ibid.*, p. 40]

Freud did not believe Anna's suicide had affected "The Wolfman" in this way, and wrote, "the patient told me, he felt hardly a trace of grief" (1918b, p. 23). Freud went on to suggest to "The Wolfman" that he was pleased his rival was now out of the way and that he would be able to inherit all the land and wealth from his father.

"The Wolfman had lived an approximately normal life during the ten years of his boyhood that preceded the date of his illness" (Freud, 1918b, p. 7). Like Freud, he had been born in a caul, and "he had for that reason always looked on himself as a special child of fortune whom no ill could befall" (*ibid.*, p. 99). At the age of four "The Wolfman" had developed an animal phobia that developed into an obsessional religious mania which continued until he was ten. His parents had both been chronically ill during his childhood, his father with depression, his mother with abdominal problems. Their illnesses meant the parents were often away seeking cures and had little to do with "The Wolfman" and his older sister in their childhood. Freud acknowledges "The Wolfman's" sister plays "an important part in his life" (*ibid.*, p.14), but I suggest it was because of the centrality he places on the role of the primal scene and the subsequent Oedipus complex, that he considers her seduction is not part of "The Wolfman's" neurosis.

"The Wolfman" was looked after by someone Freud described as "an uneducated old peasant woman" (p. 14) called Nanya. I am reminded of Freud's description of his nurse as "a prehistoric old woman" (1900a, p. 248). In the summer, when "The Wolfman" was three-and-a-half years old and his sister Anna was five-and-a-half, his parents went away and a governess was employed to help Nanya look after the two children. Either during the spring or summer of that year his sister "seduced him into sexual practices" (1918b, p. 20). The "sexual practices" consisted of showing each other their bottoms and "his sister had taken hold of his penis and played with it, at the same time telling him incomprehensible stories about his Nanya" (p. 20). When his parents came back "they found him transformed. He had become discontented, irritable and violent, took offence at every possible occasion, and then flew into a violent rage and screamed like a savage" (p. 15). Freud tells us "The Wolfman's" family gave various explanations for the change in his behaviour, and most of the blame was put on the English governess, who was dismissed. Not only had "The Wolfman's" behaviour changed but he now suffered from a fear of a picture book with a wolf that was "standing upright and striding along" (p. 16). His sister delighted in tormenting him with this picture.

"What was the origin of the sudden change in the boy's character?" Freud asks (p. 17). This is a rhetorical question that Freud answers in the following way. "It is very natural, then, to connect this transformation with the awakening of his sexual activity that had meanwhile taken place" (p. 24). However, it was not the explanation that Freud was to give. He came to a more complicated conclusion about the change in "The Wolfman's" behaviour. It needs to be borne in mind that when Freud was treating "The Wolfman" he was developing his drive theory. In this theory, he was to postulate, "An instinct ... impinges not from without but from within the organism" (1915c, p. 118).[1] This idea sits uneasily with Freud's central argument of this case, that it was "The Wolfman's" witnessing of the primal scene that was the foundation of his later neuroses, though it helps us understand why Freud had to insist that "The Wolfman's" neurosis could not be linked to his sister's seduction.

We have already seen, in the previous chapter, that by 1900 Freud no longer believed in his seduction theory, his *neurotica*. Events outside the mind are no longer as crucial in the aetiology of neuroses as the conflict between the sexual drive and its repression. Memories are now to be seen as expressions of instinctual impulses not memories of real events.

> ... psychic structures which, in hysteria, are affected by repression are not in reality memories—since no one indulges in memory activity without a motive—but *impulses*. [Masson, 1985, p. 239]

It is at this juncture that Freud brings in his concept of *nachträglichkeit* or "deferred action".[2] He had already been thinking about this idea in 1896 when he wrote to Fliess:

> I am working on the assumption that our psychical mechanism has come into being by a process of stratification: the material present in

the shape of memory traces—being subjected from time to time to a re-arrangement in accordance with fresh circumstances—is as it were, transcribed. [*ibid.*, p. 233]

In "The Wolfman" he seems to be working out the concept more fully with the idea that trauma in infancy remains repressed until some event later on in life activates an inappropriate response that is experienced as traumatic.

... (I)nfantile sexual experiences ... remain without effect to begin with and only exercise a pathogenic action later, when they have been aroused after puberty in the form of unconscious memories. [1896c, p. 212]

The question then arises as to how the gap can be filled between an infantile sexual trauma and its remembering or becoming experienced. One answer that Freud gives is to divide the mind between the sexual drive and the objects of attachment. This division allows the two impulses to float more freely, as it were, until sexual maturity is reached. It is only at the point of adolescence that the sexual drive and the object of attachment meet up and remembering becomes possible. " It seems probable that the sexual instinct is in the first instance independent of its object; nor is its origin likely to be due to its object's attractions" (1905a, p. 148).

However, Freud seems to have doubts as he works on this new model of the mind and he suddenly says about "The Wolfman", "The old trauma theory of the neuroses ... had suddenly come to the front once more" (1918b, p. 95). But, he dismisses such anxiety as soon as he reminds himself and his readers that this case was to be a good example of an infantile sexual trauma that had not registered in the psyche as a trauma until a later stage of development. And so Freud continues, "Out of critical interest I made one more attempt to *force* upon the patient another view of his story" (*ibid.*, my italics) and suggested to "The Wolfman" that he had reacted "to the allurements of his elder sister ... by a refusal which applied to the person and not to the thing" (p. 24). It seems that the distinction he is making here between "person" and "thing", is, as we have seen above, the equivalent to the distinction he is making between an object and the sexual drive. This prising apart of "person" and "thing" allows Freud to say "The Wolfman" had never desired his sister (as an object), but he had desired the "thing" (the satisfaction of his drive).

> The object of an instinct is the thing in regard to which or through which the instinct is able to achieve its aim. It is what is most *variable* about an instinct and is not *originally connected with it.* [1915c, p. 122, italics mine]

"The Wolfman" only desired the satisfaction of his impulse, he did not desire his sister, and therefore repudiated her. Nevertheless, he looked for other ways of satisfying his impulse and turned to his beloved Nanya. This time there was a different response and his Nanya rejected him and threatened him with castration. "His Nanya disillusioned him; she made a serious face, and explained that that wasn't good; children who did that, she added, got a 'wound' in the place" (1918b, p. 24). The conclusion Freud came to was that "when his fits of rage set in, it became clear that he really was embittered against her [his Nanya]" (p. 24), not his sister, as a less sophisticated theory might suppose.

In spite of the rejection by his Nanya, "The Wolfman" did not give up and he "began to look around for another sexual object. His seduction had given him the passive sexual aim of being touched on the genitals" (p. 24). To whom should he turn? Freud went on to say, "It looks as though his seduction by his sister had forced him into a passive role, and had given him a passive sexual aim" (p. 27). Freud's theory suggests that siblings and nurses, even if they have been "the child's first choice of an object ... soon give place to its parents" (1910a, p. 47). So, in conformity with this idea, Freud asserts that "The Wolfman", though he was:

> under the influence of this experience [the seduction by his sister] ... pursued a path from his sister via his Nanya to his father ... His father was now his object once more; in conformity with his higher stage of development, identification was replaced by object-choice. [1918b, p. 27]

How did Freud reach this conclusion? It might seem that when Freud says "the transformation of ... [the Wolfman's] active attitude into a passive one was the consequence and the record of the seduction which had occurred meanwhile" (p. 27), he is returning to his earlier theory of neuroses. However, had Freud rested with this conclusion, he would be giving due weight to the seduction. So, Freud goes on to suggest "The Wolfman" had suffered a trauma that had been forgotten. This earlier trauma was revealed by a dream that "The Wolfman" had had when he was three-and-a-half. The dream went as follows:

> I dreamt that it was night and that I was lying in my bed. (My bed stood with its foot towards the window; in front of the window there was a row of old walnut trees. I know it was winter when I had the dream, and night-time.) Suddenly the window opened of its own accord, and I was terrified to see that some white wolves were sitting on the big walnut tree in front of the window. There were six or seven of them. The wolves were quite white, and looked more like foxes or sheep-dogs, for they had big tails like foxes and they had their ears pricked like dogs when they pay attention to something. In great terror, evidently of being eaten up by the wolves I screamed. [p. 29]

The interpretation Freud gave was that "The Wolfman" had witnessed the primal scene when he was one-and-a-half years old and it was this experience that brought into play his passive sexual aim (p. 109). The witnessing of the primal scene was the experience that gave rise to his fear of his father. It lead also to "the wish to be born of his father ..., the wish to be sexually satisfied by him, the wish to present him with a child" (p. 101). This wish caused "The Wolfman's" "manic depressive anxiety" and "... the strongest motive for his falling ill" (p. 32). Furthermore, it was "... his ambivalent attitude towards every father-surrogate (that) was the dominating feature of his life as well as his behaviour during the treatment" (p. 32).

Freud is aware he might be stretching our credulity at this point, for he says "the reader's belief will abandon me" (p. 36.). I believe that Freud knew he was pressing the facts of the case into a mould that did not fit, emotionally or theoretically. In 1901 Fliess had apparently been critical of Freud's emerging psychoanalytic theory and suggested that Freud was a: "reader of thoughts (who) merely reads his own thoughts into other people" (Masson, 1985, p. 447). Freud's emerging theory is, of course, based upon his own self-analysis, as the letters to Fliess testify, and therefore, there is some truth to Fliess' criticism. In this famous case Freud is, I believe, still hard at work on his own neurosis, and the possibility of "the incurability of hysteria" that he mentions in connection with his nurse (Masson, 1985, p. 269). Freud knew he was explaining something beyond the facts of the case and it is for this reason that he suddenly warns the reader: "I have now reached the point at which I must abandon the support I have thitherto had from the course of the analysis. I am afraid it will also be the point at which the reader's belief will abandon me". He goes on to say:

> What sprang into activity that night out of the chaos of the dreamer's unconscious memory-traces was the picture of copulation between his parents, copulation in circumstances which were not entirely usual and were especially favourable for observation. [1918b, p. 36]

I now want to leap to one of the very last things that Freud wrote, for I think it is there that we might get a clue to Freud's anxiety that "the reader's belief will abandon me", and it may also help to explain the experience that many readers have of something being forced upon them, just as it was upon "The Wolfman". At the very end of Freud's life he was still concerned with the question of what constitutes trauma and how it manifests itself in neurosis. In *Moses and Monotheism* (1939a) he writes: "We give the name of *traumas* to those impressions, experienced and later forgotten, to which we attach such great importance in the aetiology of the neuroses" (p. 72). It might seem from that quotation that *traumas* could be manifold, but here he is quite definite that he is referring to the trauma of witnessing the primal scene. By way of illustration he takes the "single case" of:

> ... (a) little boy, who, as is so often in middle-class families, shared his parent's bedroom during the first years of his life, had repeated, and indeed regular, opportunities of observing sexual acts between his parents—of seeing some things and hearing still more—at an age when he had scarcely learnt to speak. [p.78]

The child was "prematurely aroused" by witnessing the primal scene, and as a result masturbated to exciting fantasies of attacking his mother while "identifying himself with his father" (*ibid.*). The mother threatened the child with castration if he continued this activity and the child gave up masturbating, became frightened of his father and identified with his mother. "In this modification of the Oedipus complex" (*ibid.*) the child passed through latency and "became an exemplary boy and was quite successful at school" (*ibid.*). Freud goes on to say that this boy's neurosis only broke out at adolescence, with the first nocturnal emission, and the neurosis took the form of sleep disturbance, the meaning of which was:

> a defence against the things he had experienced at night, and on the other an attempt to re-establish the waking state in which he was able to listen to those impressions. [p. 79]

But it also took the form of "sexual impotence", that is to say, he still continued to abstain from masturbation and from approaching girls, and instead resorted to "psychical masturbation accompanied by sadomasochistic phantasies" (*ibid.*) which consisted of "furious hatred of his father and insubordination . . . and . . . conflicts with the external world" (*ibid.*). "Nor did he make any friends and was never on good terms with his superiors" (pp. 79–80). At the death of his father he was able to find a wife, but at the same time discovered:

> as though they were the core of his being, character-traits which made contact with him a hard task for those about him. He developed a completely egoistic, despotic and brutal personality, which clearly felt the need to suppress and insult other people. [p. 80]

Freud ends this painful account with the comment that the man had identified with "a faithful copy of his father as he had formed a picture of him in his memory" (*ibid.*).

What I find so poignant about that "story of a single case" is that I believe Freud is giving us, at the end of his life, a brief summary of his own struggle with his own neurosis. If this is the case, we can begin to make sense of Freud's uneasiness that the reader's credulity might be stretched in the case of "The Wolfman". We might see "The Wolfman's" case as facilitating the uncovering of an unconscious memory that belonged to Freud and it was this memory that wanted to "force" itself upon "The Wolfman's" dream. I am not alone in suggesting this possibility, (Anzieu, 1986; Mahony, 1984). It is also the case that "The Wolfman" when he was interviewed in his early eighties, said that he did not sleep in his parents bedroom for: "In Russia, children sleep in their nanny's bedroom, not in their parents'" (Obholzer, 1982, p. 36).

The case history of "The Wolfman" stands more as an important witness to Freud's evolving understanding of himself, than as a history of an obsessional neurosis, and it is a case that still raises difficulties in conceptualizing a theory of instincts or drive and the impact of impressions and experiences upon the mind. There seems little evidence that Freud had any success in curing "The Wolfman's" neurosis; he returned briefly for further analysis with Freud, and then had two re-analyses with Ruth Mack Brunswick, who was herself, at the time, in analysis with Freud. Several other analyses followed after the second world war (Mahony, 1984). "The Wolfman" himself commented that Freud had "more or less dragged in by the hair" the interpretation of the dream (Obholzer, 1982, p. 51).

I want to end this chapter with the suggestion that "The Wolfman's" relationship with his sister was enormously important to him and helped to structure his internal world. Others have been of the same opinion (Bank & Kahn, 1982; Luzes, 1990; Mitchell, 2000). I would also go on to suggest that an explanation of his unsatisfactory sexual relationships with women in his adult life, needs to take into account his relationship with his sister, and his Nanya, as well as his mother. "The Wolfman" and his sister grew up together, played together and saw much more of each other than any one else and it seems inconceivable that they were not deeply dependent upon each other. The fact that incestuous fantasies were acted out in childhood and in adolescence suggests they turned to each other for the emotional nurturance they were not getting, more appropriately, elsewhere. In adolescence, "The Wolfman" tried to seduce his sister. His sister rejected his sexual advances and "... he at once turned away from her to a little peasant girl who was a servant in the house and had the same name as his sister" (1918b, p. 22). Freud goes on to say that this servant, and the many subsequent servant girls he turned to "... were substitutes for the figure of the sister whom he had to forego" (*ibid.*). Yet, Freud would have us believe that "the figure of the sister whom he had to forego" was not part of his neurosis.[3]

Notes

1. At the beginning of this paper Freud writes that the concept of "instinct" is "still somewhat obscure but ... is indispensable" (pp. 117–118). And

Strachey in his editor's note points out two difficulties in translating *Triebe* as "instinct". "Drive" or "urge" might be more accurate were it not for the fact that Freud also wants the concept of *Trieb* to hold, as it were, the further idea of *Triebreprasentanz* or "instinct representation".

2. I am indebted to Kirsty Hall's exposition of Freud's concept of *nachträglikeit* in an unpublished paper, "Nachträglichkeit—an exploration of its place in the thinking of Freud, Lacan and Laplanche".

3. See Freud's paper on Jensen's *Gradiva*, (1907a). In his autobiography (1925d, p. 5) he spoke contemptuously of this work as having "no particular merit in itself". However, as I am arguing throughout this book, I believe Freud was turning his back on a competing theory of mind which Jensen's work represented, that relationships amongst children can determine later choices of sexual partners. For those not familiar with the paper, I will give a brief synopsis. Freud, encouraged by Jung, had read Jensen's tale of *Gradiva*, and used it to illustrate the way in which the mind can repress painful or conflictual desires, which nevertheless return in the form of hallucinations. In this case, the hero of the tale, a lover and collector of antiquities, makes a journey on his own to Naples. He is enamoured of an Etruscan painting of a young woman and the way in which her left leg had been painted. He is walking through the city and sees a young woman and imagines it is the young girl from the painting. He pursues her and they talk. They agree to meet next day. The love affair continues, with the reader left in some confusion as to who this young lady might be. Finally, the denouement is arrived at and we discover that the young lady in question is not a reincarnation of the Etruscan painting, but a girl from the hero's childhood with whom, it is implied, there had been a sexual relationship. Freud's interest in the tale had been to show the return of repressed wishes, through the form of hallucination. I want to suggest that alongside that insight we need to take into account the nature of the wish. The wish was for the young girl of the hero's childhood. This wish had an overriding effect upon the hero's sexual development. It is this wish that I want to suggest is a threat to Freud's theory of the Oedipus complex, unless the place of the young girl is assumed to represent the mother.

CHAPTER FIVE

Klein and siblings

"The feminine!—Perhaps it is dawning on you how deeply I have drunk from this cup and drowned myself in it in order to reap my pleasure from its gay and foamy brim. Only one other person knows about [it], and what he knows is wrong, for he had treacherously expelled it from me with his own loving ways"

Grosskurth, 1985, p. 24

I ended the previous chapter with a suggestion that Freud had turned his back upon "The Wolfman's" attachment to his sister, for it came into conflict with his emerging drive theory and the centrality he was to place on the Oedipus complex. The result has been that psychoanalytic theory has relegated siblings to an insignificant place in the internal world. It was with great surprise I discovered that Klein, in early writings, holds a very challenging view on siblings and their importance in psychic development. I say surprise, because if my understanding of these ideas about sibling relationships is correct, it seems that, in 1926, Klein is theoretically repositioning herself with the early Freud, of

1895, before he had developed his drive theory and the Oedipus complex. It also needs to be noted that, though I am in agreement with some of the ideas Klein has about siblings and their emotional significance to each other, Klein's later model of the mind is not one that I use in my clinical practice.

The opening quotation comes from a letter that Klein's older brother, Emmanuel, sent her in 1901 following her engagement to Arthur Klein.[1] Emmanuel was twenty-four at the time and Melanie was nineteen. Grosskurth (1985) says that it was "a puzzling, incoherent passage which seems to refer to Melanie and her intended husband" (p. 24). It is clear from a letter that Melanie's mother wrote to Emmanuel in that same year, 1901, that Melanie and Emmanuel had a very close relationship. The letter begins, "My dear and beloved child, I must tell you that your relationship with Melanie has often filled me with jealousy". She then goes on, as if to reassure herself, "I believe, my dear child, that there is no bond, be that of friendship or of love, that is as strong and powerful as that of mother-love" (*ibid.*, p. 24). Emmanuel knew he was dying, as did all his family, when he wrote the letter with the "puzzling incoherent passage" to Melanie. He had had scarlet fever and rheumatic fever as a child, which had affected his heart. He had later developed tuberculosis and in 1901 he was travelling in Southern Italy in search of warmth and sunshine. He died eighteen months later in Genoa. Many years later Klein wrote in her autobiography that Emmanuel was "the best friend I ever had" (quoted in Grosskurth, 1985, p. 39). Grosskurth goes further than that and says, "Brother and sister, they were twin souls, sharing the same sorts of moods and reactions. He was her surrogate father, close companion, phantom lover—and no one in her life was ever able to replace him" (p. 39).

In the previous chapters, I suggested that Freud's feelings about his own siblings need to be taken into account if we wish to understand why siblings have been ignored in psychoanalytic theory. In this chapter, I shall argue that we need to bear in mind the significance of Klein's relationship with her brother, Emmanuel, as we track through her complex ideas on the passions that accompany sibling love and hate.

In her early writing, Klein (1932) is quite certain of the efficacy of sibling love on the developing psyche and she puts much greater emphasis upon its importance than does Freud. This idea is in marked contrast to the way she thinks about the relationship between parents and children, for there we see her firmly held Freudian belief that "hatred ... (is) the basis of object relations ... with ... parents" (*ibid.*, p. 135n). Her sympathy for siblings leads her to suggest that they promote emotional development and help in the task of distancing the child from its parents. She does not deny sibling rivalry and jealousy, but these emotions only play a part in the experience between siblings and are not the essential bedrock upon which the relationship is built. Sibling love is crucially important and a failure to be loved by or to love peers and siblings can emotionally distort later relationships. Unlike Freud she does not believe that strong sibling involvement is necessarily the consequence of a "faithless mother" (Freud, 1916–1917).

Klein makes an interesting distinction between sibling incestuous attachment and oedipal conflict. She writes that: "The existence of sexual relations between children in early life, especially between brothers and sisters, is a very common occurrence" (1932, p. 223). Oedipal conflict, by contrast, may have incestuous wishes at its heart, but it is not fuelled by wishes for sexual relations between parents and children, indeed quite the opposite: "... it is chiefly impulses of hate which initiate the Oedipus conflict" (*ibid.*, p. 135). She says her view is in line with Freud's drive theory that "Hate as a relation to objects, is older than love. It derives from the narcissistic ego's primordial repudiation of the external world with its outpouring of the stream of stimuli" (Freud, 1915c, p. 139; *ibid.*, p. 135). In a footnote, she elaborates further:

> My own view that the Oedipus conflict starts under the primacy of sadism seems to me to supplement what Freud says since it gives another reason why hatred should be the basis of object-relationships in the fact that the child forms its relation with its parents—a relationship that is so fundamental and so decisive for all its future object-relationships—during the time when its sadistic trends are at their height. [1932, p. 135]

It is precisely because of the fact that Klein believes that, "it is impulses of hate that initiate the Oedipus conflict" (*ibid.*) that she counterbalances this hatred with sibling love. Children need to love and it is through the companionship of their siblings and peers that the envy and jealousy of the maternal breast can be repaired and the unbearable exclusion from the parental bed can be mitigated.

There is, however, something more complicated and challenging in Klein's thinking on siblings. She cites many cases of destructive sexual relations between siblings. For instance, Peter and his younger brother engaged "at a very early age ... (in) sexual acts" (*ibid.*, p. 182). In another case Gunther and Franz engaged in "mutual *fellatio*, masturbation and touching the anus with the fingers" as a result of "overwhelming anxiety and guilt" about their parents' sexual intercourse (*ibid.*, p. 113–117). And again Ilse and Gert were brother and sister who engaged in "coitus like acts" in early adolescence, and in earlier childhood they had also had sexual relations (*ibid.*, pp. 117–118). Mr B and his two brothers had sexual relationships from early childhood and practised *fellatio*. The unconscious phantasies that Mr B was enacting were towards the "imagos of the magical "good" penis (his father) and of the terrifying mother" (*ibid.*, pp. 267–268). In all of these cases Klein stresses that the sexual relationship between the siblings had been destructive, because sexual activities had been fuelled by excessively sadistic "phantasies" towards the parents in sexual intercourse. These "phantasies" produced strong masturbatory guilt and the result was that their guilt was too strong to allow the children to give up their sexual activities. For instance, Gunther and Franz, the brothers who had engaged in sexual activities from the ages of three and two respectively, were trapped in their sexual relationship because Gunther was driven by a wish to put his brother to death, and at the same time, Franz unconsciously knew of Gunther's wish and believed that their behaviour would prevent his death. Klein takes the view that it is the wish for and the fear of the death of the parents in sexual intercourse, that lay behind their sexual activities.

In spite of the destructive effect that sexual relationships can have upon children, Klein believes sexual relationships between children are the rule and are not necessarily destructive.

> In general, as regards the existence of sexual relations between children, especially between brothers and sisters, ... They are the *rule* in early childhood ... Furthermore, although early experiences like these can do a lot of harm in some cases, in others they may influence the child's general development favourably. For besides satisfying the child's libido and his desire for sexual knowledge

relations of this kind serve the important function of reducing his
excessive sense of guilt ... the fact that his proscribed phantasies
against his parents are shared by a partner gives him the feeling of
having an ally and this greatly lightens the burden of his anxiety.

She ends the passage by saying:

From my knowledge of a number of cases, I should say that where
the positive and libidinal factors predominate, such a relationship
has a favourable influence upon the child's object relations and
capacity to love. [*ibid.*, pp. 118–119, my italics]

She elaborated these ideas further in the same book in her
chapter, "The sexual development of the girl".

Where an excessive fear of both parents, together with certain
external factors, would have produced an Oedipus situation which
would have prejudiced her attitude towards the opposite sex and
greatly hampered her in the maintenance of her feminine position
and her ability to love, the fact that she had sexual relations with a
brother or brother-substitute in early childhood and that that
brother has also shown real affection for her and been her protector,
has provided the basis for a heterosexual position in her and
developed her capacity for love. [p. 223]

This radical idea shifts the resolution of the Oedipus complex in an
interesting way. Klein seems to be saying that it is possible for a girl
to have a difficult oedipal relationship with her parents, to the
extent that it could be prejudicial to developing a normal sexual
relationship in adult life. However, should the girl have a sexual
relationship with a brother, or brother-substitute, this can restore
her capacity to love and to be heterosexual. The factor that makes
the sexual relationship between siblings "good" as opposed to
"destructive", is the degree of sadism between the two children. If it
is not excessive, the relationship can only increase the capacity to
love. Klein gives a clinical case of a girl who "had had two types of
love-object, one representing the stern father and the other the kind
brother". And she goes on to say: "In serving as a proof grounded
upon reality of the existence of the 'good' penis, the girl's relations
with her brother fortify her belief in the 'good' introjected penis and
moderate her fear of 'bad' introjected objects" (*ibid.*, pp. 223–224). In

other words, the girl's capacity to love can be the result of her sexual relationship with her brother.

This positive sexual relationship, that children can have with each other, Klein goes on to say, can give them the feeling of being, "in league ... against ... (the) parents". This "secret complicity" relieves the children of their deepest anxiety about their, "sadistic masturbatory phantasies that were originally directed at their mother and father" for they have now become "accomplices in crime" (*ibid.*, p. 224). But, lest we should look askance at the link she wants to make between positive sexual relationships between siblings and being "accomplices in crime", she adds, as if to normalize what she has claimed, "the existence of a secret complicity of this sort ... plays an essential part in *every* relationship of love, even, between grown-up people" (p. 224, my italics).

Klein is saying that children can have a real sexual relationship with each other and that it can be a good thing. In particular, it is a good thing when there has been excessive hatred of the parents. By a sexual relationship, I do not think Klein means the exploration of genitals that most children engage in. When she refers to the sexual relationship between siblings, she speaks of "mutual sexual activities" (*ibid.*, p. 223), and "performing sexual acts" (*ibid.*, p. 224). It seems more likely she is describing the active engagement in *fellatio*, mutual masturbation, anal fingering and coital-like acts, as in the earlier pathological cases. If that is what she means, it is a challenging idea. It is challenging because it does seem to suggest that we can find a way around facing oedipal conflict with parents if they have been too disappointing, should we have the good fortune to have a sibling who does not wish to dominate us. But even more controversially, Klein seems to be of the opinion that "... if ... (the) Oedipus objects have not become good imagos" (*ibid.*, p. 222) or if the phantasy of the parental couple in sexual congress arouses too much sadism then it *requires* a loving sibling sexual relationship to restore the "good" penis inside.

I think that most people would find it difficult to go along with Klein's ideas about active sibling incestuous love and I shall be looking at some of these difficulties in the next chapter. However, her idea about the important part that sibling love can play in emotional development does much to redress a balance that has been lost in Freud. Siblings are now placed as possible facilitators of mental health and as essential secret allies against the terrifying world of parents in sexual intercourse. Even more radical is the idea that it can be through brotherly love and identification with our siblings that we achieve adult heterosexuality, rather than through an identification with our parents. We may not be prepared to go along with the idea that sexual relations with siblings can facilitate later heterosexual development, but this idea of Klein's does challenge the "classical" psychoanalytic assumption that sibling/peer relationships are essentially held in the quicksand of rivalry for parental love. Furthermore, if successful adult sexual attachment involves the "secret complicity" of sibling sexual attachment, then we need to reconsider the theory that it is only through the resolution of our sexual desires for our parents that sexual maturity is achieved.

I began this chapter with a quotation from a letter that Emanuel had sent Melanie soon after he had heard of her engagement. It becomes clear from Grosskurth's biography of Melanie Klein that the relationship between brother and sister was extremely strong and important to them both. I think, in the early works of Klein, we see her struggling with her belief in the importance of Freud and his psychoanalytic theory. She believes in the Oedipus complex and that "hate as a relation to objects is older than love" (Freud, 1915c, p. 139), yet her experience with Emmanuel tells her something different. "He was my confidant, my friend, my teacher" (Grosskurth, 1985, p. 16). The conflict in her theory about infant sexual development is palpable. The significance in all that early Klein has said about sibling relationships, is that it restores siblings to a place in the inner world, where they have always been, even if psychoanalytic theory has been reluctant to acknowledge this.

It is quite striking to compare early Klein with George Eliot, another writer who wrote on passionate sibling attachment. George Eliot wrote a poem called *Brother and Sister* (1896). It is not a poetic masterpiece, but it keenly portrays George Eliot's belief that the childhood love she had for her brother Isaac informed her later loves and attachment (Redinger, 1976).

Thus rambling we were schooled in deepest lore,
And learned the meanings that give words a soul,
The fear, the love, the primal passionate store,
Whose shaping impulses make manhood whole. [p. 213]

In 1873 George Eliot wrote to her publisher, John Blackwood, about this poem which she had written four-years earlier. She said it was "on the childhood of a brother and sister—little descriptive bits on the mutual influence in their small lives. *This was always one of my best loved subjects*" (Redinger, 1976, p. 44, my emphasis). The poem goes on to say that through the time brother and sister spent together, "Those hours were seed to all my after good" (p. 213). I think that both Melanie Klein and George Eliot would agree that whatever the subsequent fate of their adult relationship with their brothers, the seed-time of their capacity to love other men was laid down in the love they held for these siblings.

Note

1. Klein later wrote, "I often wonder whether my brother, with whom I had such a deep and close connection, did not realize that I was doing the wrong thing, and whether he did not unconsciously know that I was going to make myself unhappy" (Grosskurth, 1985, p. 41).

CHAPTER SIX

Sibling sexual relationships

"12th November 1599.
There is much talk of the tragical death of Mistress Ratcliffe, the Maid of Honour, who ever since the death of Sir Alexander her brother hath pined in such strange manner as voluntarily she hath gone about to starve herself, and by the two days together hath received not sustenance, which meeting with extreme grief had made an end of her maiden modest days at Richmond yesterday. Her Majesty commanded her body to be opened, and it was found well and sound, saving certain strings striped all over her heart"

G. B. Harrison, 1955, ii, 49/50

Mistress Ratcliffe was one of Elizabeth I's Maids of Honour. She was buried in Westminster Cathedral, and it was said that her death was much talked about in Shakespeare's London (Harrison, 1955). The question people asked was: what was the nature of the relationship she had with her brother?

I ended the previous chapter with a suggestion that early Klein reinstates siblings into the inner world and redresses a balance that gets lost if the Oedipus complex is seen as the exclusive foundation for adult desire. The more difficult question is her claim that sexual relations between children "may influence the child's general development favourably" (Klein, 1932, p. 118).

Klein is not alone in addressing sibling sexual relationships. Many of the foundation myths of ancient civilizations have involved sibling incest. For instance, biblical commentators have suggested that Cain fought Abel over Abel's twin sister, who had been given to Abel in marriage (Luzes, 1990). Abraham married his sister, Sarah (Graves & Patai, 1966, p. 88). Zeus married his sister, Hera, and his sister, Demeter (Graves, 1955). Geb married his twin sister, Nut (Raphael-Leff, 1990). We can see that sibling incest has held a strong place in cultural myths about the beginning of the world and is a potent part of our imaginative heritage.

At the present time, we do not have much evidence relating to the prevalence of sibling incest or its effects for, as Bank and Kahn (1982) point out: " There is, to our knowledge, *no* evidence in the literature, or in our sample, of sexual play between very young (under six years old) siblings of the same sex" (note, p. 155). I need to make clear that, when I talk of sibling incest, I am not referring to the sort of sex play that is defined as, "activities of young children of the same age, engaged in mutually, that are limited to the showing and touching of genitals, and that go on for a short period of time" (Finkelhor, 1980, p. 172) I am referring to: "the existence of sexual relations ... especially between brothers and sisters ... (that) satisfy the child's libido and his desire for sexual knowledge" (Klein, 1932, p. 118–119).

Klein is referring here to a sexual relationship between prepubescent children. This needs distinguishing from a sexual relationship between siblings that continues into adolescence and adulthood, which, as we shall see, is much more rare. Klein (1932) suggested that the effect upon the psyche of pre-adolescent incest was determined by the intentions of the children involved. If there was mutual love and consent, the act was not damaging. Marie Bonaparte (1953) was also of the view that sibling incest, for the girl, might be:

a corrective to ... oedipal frustration, as well as teaching her to change her object and return to lovers of her own age, which is biologically desirable, since every succeeding generation must make its life together. In the same way, the sister, as a substitute for that unsatisfactory initiator into sexuality, the oedipal mother, may play an analogous part for her little brother. [p. 136]

As recently as 1990, Ascherman and Safier quoted three authors who suggested that, "sibling incest may be less pathological than other forms or may not be harmful at all" (p. 311).

Both may willingly engage in the behaviour as an attempt to cope with unmet needs. Such needs may include a desire for affiliation and affection; a combating of loneliness, depression, and a sense of isolation; and a discharging of anxiety and tension due to stress. [Ascherman and Safier, p. 178; a quotation from Loredo (1982) on the works of Nakashima & Zakus (1979), Riemer (1940), Weeks (1976)]

There seems to be a common agreement between the three authors quoted in Ascherman and Safier and the views of Klein and Bonaparte, that sibling sexual relationships may ease oedipal conflict, combat loneliness, and encourage sexually appropriate behaviour. They all stress that it is the motives behind the behaviour that determine the nature of the act. If there is a wish by one sibling to gain power and control over the other, then the relationship is damaging and abusive.

However, there is something more difficult and complex in Klein's belief that an incestuous relationship between brother and sister can provide: "the basis for a heterosexual position in ... (the girl) and develop her capacity for love" (Klein, 1932, p. 223), if there has been "an excessive fear of both parents" (*ibid.*). A distinction needs to be made between the close emotional support that siblings and peers give each other when lonely or engaged in a difficult oedipal battle, such as George Eliot is describing in *Mill on the Floss* or in her poem *Brother and Sister*, and children engaging in active sexual behaviour. Entertaining fantasies is qualitatively different to acting them out. But with both Klein and Bonaparte this distinction becomes blurred. Furthermore, it is not clear whether the "the secret complicity" of siblings is not only easing oedipal conflict, but also by-passing it.

The Freudian resolution of the Oedipus complex requires an acknowledgement of our unconscious wishes to murder the parent of the opposite sex and marry the other, and then the further renunciation of these wishes through identification with the parent of the same sex. On one reading, both Klein and Bonaparte imply that there is a way of evading a particular sort of oedipal difficulty caused by "excessive fear of both parents" (Klein, 1932, p. 223). In cases such as these, a girl's sexual development may be "greatly hampered in her maintenance of her feminine position and her ability to love" (*ibid*.). If she has a brother or brother-substitute, with whom she can have an affectionate sexual relationship, then her heterosexual development is restored. It is this conclusion that is difficult to square with the oedipal task as laid out by Freud. It seems to me that such a relationship, which Klein acknowledges as a "secret complicity ... in league ... against ... parents" (p. 223), directly interferes with the task of facing "the excessive fear of both parents" (*ibid*.).

If pre-adolescent children are engaged in a sexual relationship, we have to take into account the fact that there will be sexual fantasies that are being enacted.

Let us say that the fantasy might be: "I wish my brother's penis was inside me". If this fantasy is then concretely enacted, the girl will have other and perhaps more perplexing experiences. If the thesis is correct that we all find it difficult to reconcile ourselves to our parents' sexual relationship (Klein, 1932), the little girl might come to believe that she can have what her parents have, now, at this moment, and gratification is not deferred until she is at a more appropriate age. In this case the little girl is bypassing her oedipal task, and avoiding the terrifying parents.

A more challenging reading of Klein and Bonaparte might be to say that they are pointing out, in contradistinction to Freud, that the oedipal resolution is not the way we establish our capacity to express our sexual desire. Instead, it is through "the secret complicity of siblings" and our identification with them, that we find our sexual identity. I want to leave that idea unanswered for the moment, and return to the question as to why sibling incest occurs.

We have already seen, in Klein, the idea that sibling incest can occur when there is "excessive fear of both parents" (1932, p. 223), and Ascherman and Safier (1990) take the view that it seems to occur when children are neglected. What is clear is that: "Sex between siblings is a phenomenon that remains poorly understood and infrequently researched" (*ibid.*, p. 311). There are few cases of sibling incest that have been recorded in the psychoanalytic journals, and they are necessarily dealing with pathology and the destructive effect of incest, such as in Reich (1935).

Bank and Kahn (1982) stand out as an exception. In their book, *The Sibling Bond*, they devote a chapter to this topic. In their view, sibling incest is dramatically under-reported, it occurs more frequently than parent–child incest, and when it is reported, three quarters of the people who report it are women. Their underlying thesis is that brother and sister incest has played a potent part in myth and literature because it describes, psychologically, a failure of parental care and attention. The children's need for affection and attachment have not been met, and as a result, they have had to turn to each other. Sibling incest involves the search for a more primitive merged state, but its consequence is always traumatic. There was one exception, a young woman of twenty-two who had a short, incestuous relationship with her brother of twenty-seven, when her marriage had broken up and she was feeling "profound loneliness and powerlessness in her life" (p. 168). From this one case they concluded that "certain adult women are able to undergo this experience without trauma" (p. 169).

It seems, therefore, that, although sibling incest is grossly under-reported[1] and there is almost no account of it in the psychoanalytic journals, we could suggest that sibling incest is linked to a deep loneliness within the children involved, which may stem from parental neglect.

The incestuous relationship between Byron and his half-sister, Augusta, would be a good example to support the thesis that sibling incest occurs as the result of parental neglect. Their relationship would also seem to support Bank and Kahn's view that some forms of sibling incest, especially between consenting adults, may be felt, by those who engage in it, to cause no trauma. Byron's incestuous relationship with his half sister, Augusta Leigh, began when they got to know each other as adults (Grosskurth, 1997).[2] They had been raised separately even though Augusta and Byron shared the same father, "Mad Jack" Byron. Augusta's mother was his first wife, who died giving birth to Augusta in 1784.[3] The following year "Mad Jack" married Catherine Gordon, a Scottish heiress and Byron was born in 1788. Two years later "Mad Jack" left his second wife and child and went to live in an incestuous relationship with a sister in France. "Mad Jack" did not see his son or daughter again and died of consumption in 1792. Augusta, meanwhile, was passed around from pillar to post, first to her uncle in France and then to her maternal grandmother in England. Byron and his mother lived, meanwhile, in Aberdeen. Byron and Augusta seem to have made contact with each other in 1802, when Augusta would have been eighteen and Byron fourteen. In 1807 Augusta married her first cousin, George Leigh, son of Frances Leigh, the sister with whom Mad Jack had been having an incestuous relationship in France. It was not until the death of Byron's mother in 1811 that the relationship between half-brother and sister began to become more intense. It became an incestuous one in 1813. Grosskurth suggested that each saw in the other an idealized figure. In Augusta's case, she saw Byron as her wayward and inconstant father, and Byron saw, in Augusta, an idealized mother. A year after their sexual relationship had begun, Augusta gave birth to a daughter, Elizabeth Medora. Byron, writing to Lady Melbourne, after the birth, declaimed, "Oh! But it is 'worth while'—I can't tell you why— and it is *not* an 'Ape'[4] ... I have been all my life trying to make someone love me—and never got the sort I preferred before" (p. 192). They attempted to conceal their relationship through Byron's marriage to Annabella Millbanke, but when Annabella left Byron a year after their marriage, the incestuous relationship was suspected and Byron left England for the rest of his life. The suspicion about their incestuous relationship was confirmed for many people when, in 1817, Byron wrote,

> She was like me in lineaments—her eyes,
> Her hair, her features, all, to the very tone
> Even of her voice, they were like to mine;
> But soften'd all, and temper'd into beauty;
> She had the same lone thoughts and wanderings ...
> And tenderness—but that I had for her. [Manfred, II, ii, 105]

Byron and Augusta had appallingly fractured childhoods and very little parental support as they grew up. It is my view that the need for a sexual relationship with a sibling, at any age, grows on the backdrop of parental neglect and abandonment. There seems to be evidence that sibling incest in adult life is more likely to occur if the siblings have not known each other in childhood (Harris, 1999). There are, of course, exceptions to this generalization, most especially in literature, for instance, Helen Dunmore's (1996) *A Spell of Winter* or Byatt's (1992) *Angels & Insects*. Nevertheless, what does seem to remain constant, in all the cases that I have read about sibling incest, is that the siblings are looking for something that is felt to be missing. "The Wolfman" and his sister, as we saw in Chapter Four, were frequently left together while their parents sought health cures. Their sexual games were probably a direct consequence of their loneliness.

Sibling incest and parental abandonment seem to go hand-in-hand. However, the experience of sibling incest, by those who engage in it with loving cooperation, is most often described as beneficial. Byron and Augusta, "The Wolfman", Melanie Klein, and Marie Bonaparte, all, in their different ways, assert that sibling incest provides love, and, furthermore, that its consequences are not damaging to those who are involved. In the cases of the "Wolfman" and Byron, both insisted that their relationships with their sisters were the most important ones in their lives.

It may be that sibling incest is more common than we have suspected. Is it less damaging to the psyche than parent/child incest, as the tale of Oedipus, or Melanie Klein would suggest? I do not have any clinical or theoretical evidence to explore this idea, and so I am going to turn to literature to try and find an answer to the question. I am not alone in using literature when the clinical material is not available. Otto Rank in 1914, writing about the idea of *The Dopplegänger*, said we might have to resort to "tracing the related forms of the motif in literary models" if we felt that there were "psychological events" that called "our attention" (Rank, 1989, p. 7).

It is rare to find parent/child incest a major theme in literature. It is far more common to find tales or hints of sibling incest; for instance, Ford *Tis Pity She's a Whore* (1633), Mann *The Holy Sinner* (1951), Musil *The Man without Qualities* (1930–1932), Nabokov *Ada* (1971). An exception to the seeming inhibition in writing on parent/child incest is *The Invisible Worm* by Jennifer Johnston (1999), in which Johnston is clearly wishing to convey to the reader that incest between a parent and child is irremediably damaging, as the title suggests.

We are introduced to the heroine, Laura, with the opening words: "I stand by the window and watch the woman running. Is it Laura? . . . I am Laura" (p. 1). The reader experiences her confusion as Laura moves between first person and third person narrative. We try to catch the nature of her suffering, and the novel ends with the words: "Laura, She will not run again. The Woman. Whoever she may be. Away. Never again . . ." (p. 181). We learn that what Laura has run away from is the memory of the seduction by her father, one hot summer day, when she was an adolescent. Chaos and destruction had followed. Laura's mother committed suicide when Laura told her and Laura is left with nothing. In some ways this novel is a good comment on the post-Freudian culture that we live in. That is to say, we believe that the restoration of memory helps to heal the damaged psyche. Laura becomes less disorientated and less split when she is helped to remember and face the incest, through her friendship with an ex-priest Dominic. However, the reader is left in no doubt about the psychic destruction that followed from the incestuous encounter with her father. Therefore, I want to suggest that this novel illustrates the intuitive belief that parent/child incest severs the psychic structure of the child *tout court*.

By contrast, Dunmore's subtle novel about brother and sister incest, in *A Spell of Winter*, leaves the reader with a heroine whose inner landscape is less bleak. Dunmore is psychologically right, I believe, to predicate the incest in this novel upon the abandonment and neglect of parents. Rob and his younger sister, Catherine, are deserted by their mother and sometime later their father goes mad and dies. They are intensely lonely and lost and yet they find warmth in their attachment to each other. The nature of this warmth changes dramatically as they move into adolescence and they have to face the potential loss of this attachment. They experience sexual desire and jealousy in their relationship to each other and with others. How can their passions be negotiated and their relationship remain intact? They falter and the leitmotiv of winter reoccurs as their first incestuous encounter takes place in a snow house they build.

The consummation of their sexual desire has destructive consequences: Rob has a riding accident, and later in the novel he is killed in the Second World War. Catherine aborts Rob's child that she is carrying. Yet, in spite of all this, we are not left at the end of the novel with a sense that Catherine's psyche has been shattered, as was the case with Laura, in *The Invisible Worm*.

The novel ends with Catherine falling in love with George and finding her mother again. In other words, though the brother/sister incest was destructive, it did not leave the devastation that Laura had experienced, nor the blighted landscape that blind Oedipus travelled across. Why is that? Dunmore has Catherine exclaim at the height of her sexual relationship with Rob: "We are turning into one another". What is the nature of this fantasy? The most common psychoanalytic interpretation would be to suggest that this is a wish to return to a fantasy of a pre-oedipal fusion with the mother.

Could the answer to Catherine's fantasy be a paradoxical one? Catherine's wish, and indeed Rob's as well, might be to return to "our mother's womb" where they played together. But, the acting out of this wish in their incestuous relationship leaves both participants less damaged than either Oedipus or Laura. Klein's answer would be that if there is no coercion or wish to have power over the other then, in pre-adolescence at the very least, it can be fulfilling and can enrich the capacity to love. What Klein's account leaves out is that, in all the cases considered in this chapter and in the chapter on "The Wolfman", sibling sexual relationships are linked to parental abandonment or neglect.

I think we need to prise apart sibling incestuous desire and actual sibling incest. Klein is making an important claim when she suggests that the "secret complicity" of incestuous desire between siblings "plays an essential part in every relationship of love, even, between grown-up people" (1975, p. 224). It also seems to be the case, if we compare the myth of Oedipus, or the two stories that I have considered above, that sibling incest leaves the psyche less devastated than parent/child incest. So, though I am not arguing for sibling incest, I do want to suggest that the capacity to experience sibling desire may enrich our capacity for mature sexual fulfilment.

Notes

1. There is a shortage of evidence about sibling incest, However, a recent NSPCC report (Child Maltreatment in the United Kingdom, 2000) dealt with abuse. This was a survey that was conducted on children between

the ages of eighteen and twenty-four, and the sample consisted of 1,235 men and 1,634 women. The response rate was higher in women. However, the authors weighted the data to correct this, as well as "regional differences and for the proportion living in households where more than one person would have been eligible", so that they could conclude that their "findings are representative of the total UK population of eighteen and twenty-four year olds" (p. 7). It revealed that: "3% of children had been sexually abused by relatives other than their parents or carers" (p. 86). "The most likely relative to abuse within the family is a brother (mentioned in a third (31%) of cases where relatives were involved.)" (p. 96). Parents and carers accounted for one percent of sexual abuse (p. 85). The criterion of sexual abuse was non-consensual sexual contact, under the age of twelve, with someone five-years-older or more. Small though this NSPCC report is, it is significant that one conclusion to be drawn from this report is that sibling incest is more common than any other type of under age sexual contact. The NSPCC chose a five-year age difference as the yardstick to define sibling sexual abuse. Children who were separated by a gap of up to four years were not deemed to be perpetrating an abusive act.

2. Grosskurth's (1997) book was based upon her research into the letters of Byron's wife and family, known as the Lovelace Papers.

3. Augusta's mother was Lady Amelia D'Arcy, wife of the Marquis of Carmarthen. She was seduced by "Mad Jack", married him in 1779 and died giving birth to Augusta in 1784.

4. A medieval belief was that the child of an incestuous union would be an ape (Grosskurth, 1997, p. 192).

CHAPTER SEVEN

Brotherly love

I n this chapter, I am going to explore the idea that there can be non-incestuous love between siblings that gives to each a support that alters their whole way of relating to others in adult life, and that we impoverish our understanding of this "primal passionate store" (Eliot, 1896) if we dismiss it as pathological or a mere "second edition" of an earlier love of child and parent (Colonna & Newman, 1983).

A concept that is absent from the psychoanalytic literature is the idea of "brotherly love". Brotherly love is associated with the idea of brotherhood: that is to say, a group of men who come together through a shared interest. A shared trauma, such as war, brings out the idea of brotherly love most strongly.

> We few, we happy few, we band of brothers;
> For he today that sheds his blood with me
> Shall be my brother. [Shakespeare, Henry V, iv, iii]

It seems that to be called someone's brother, in this context, is high praise. The *Shorter Oxford Dictionary* defines "brotherliness" as a "friendly alliance ... community of feeling uniting man and man", and "brotherly" as a "characteristic of a brother, kind, affectionate, hence brotherliness". What becomes clear from these quotations is that brothers are assumed to love each other and that to attribute "brotherly love" to people, who are not related, is to give their relationship a special importance. I think it is also assumed that "brotherly love" is a non-sexual love.

When it comes to "sisterhood", there does not seem to be a concept of "sisterly love".[1] But nevertheless as with the concept of "brotherhood", "sisterhood" is often associated with a group of women who come together for religious purposes, such as the Sisters of Charity. The concept of "sister" is also associated to someone who looks after others, such as "a head nurse in a hospital" (*Webster*). When it comes to the concept of "sisterly", it is defined as "like or becoming a sister; affectionate" (*Webster*). There seems to be a common assumption, with both the concepts of "brotherhood" and "sisterhood", that the love between brothers is affectionate and the same is true for the love between sisters. The love between brother and sister is not picked out within a dictionary definition as having a special aspect or quality, but what the concepts of "brotherhood" and "sisterhood" help to make clear is that we have a common-sense idea of "brotherly love". It can be strong and important, it can be a compliment if it is attributed to one's peer, and above all, it is a love that is different from the love of parents and children.

As I have already said the concept of "brotherly love" is not to be found in psychoanalytic theory. The nearest that one gets to such an idea is in Freud's (1921c) paper on "Group Psychology". The basic premise of the paper is that a group feeling begins in the nursery and that it is hostile. The older child will be envious of the younger one and wish to get rid of it. However, when the older child sees the parents' love for the younger child, he or she feels forced to identify with the younger one. In other words, for Freud, cooperative and loving feelings between siblings are always a "reaction-formation" (*ibid.*, p. 120). The "reaction-formation", in time, creates a "group spirit" or "esprit de corps" (*ibid.*, p. 120). These feelings are derived from envy that has been transformed into social justice. "If I can't have it, neither shall you", is the sentiment that lies behind the seemingly cooperative behaviour of social groups and therefore, by implication, of "brotherly love".

I have already suggested that Freud's negative view about siblings may be linked to his own experience. I have also suggested that his oedipal theory erases the important role siblings may have in emotional development. I argue that we put a stranglehold on the richness of our emotional life if sibling attachment and love is reduced to a "second edition" of the original parental relationship (Colonna and Newman, 1983).

Wordsworth wrote that his sister Dorothy, "... gave me eyes, ... gave me ears", (Woof, 1991). It has been suggested, by some writers, that Dorothy and William's intense relationship was linked to the loss of their mother (Britton, 1998; Darbishire, 1958). Dorothy and William, as in many cases of strong sibling attachment, incestuous or otherwise, had suffered loss and abandonment. Their mother died when Dorothy was six and William was eight. Dorothy left the family home and was brought up by her mother's cousin. She scarcely saw her three older brothers until she was grown up and she never returned to the parental home again. Her father died when she was twelve. In 1795, when she was twenty-three and William was twenty-five, they set up home and lived together for the rest of their lives, even though William married in 1802. Darbishire (1958) in her introduction to Dorothy's *Journals* believes that Dorothy took the place of a mother for William. Dorothy's *Journal* testifies to the solicitousness of her concern for his health and well-being. But is that all Dorothy was for William? And who was William for Dorothy?

For instance, on 15th April 1802, Dorothy wrote about some daffodils they had seen when they had taken a walk together.

> I never saw daffodils so beautiful they grew among the mossy stones about & about them, some rested their heads upon these stones as on a pillow for weariness & the rest tossed & reeled & danced & seemed as if they verily laughed with the wind that blew upon them over the Lake, they looked so gay ever glancing ever changing. [Woof, 1991, p. 85]

Two years later, in 1804 Wordsworth wrote his famous poem about daffodils: "Tossing their heads in sprightly dance" (Poems of the Imagination, XII). There is evidence that Wordsworth used to read Dorothy's *Journal*, (Gittings & Manton, 1988) and in this case it seems clear that it was Dorothy's eyes and ears that provided not only the emotion, but also some of the words of Wordsworth's poem (Darbishire, 1958; Woof, 1991).

I am trying to tease out the question as to whether there is a quality of sibling love that we have not quite captured, if we can only see the Wordsworths' relationship as replacing their dead parents. Dorothy was present for William in a way that no mother could have been. William was able to use Dorothy's observations for his poetry, that would have been impossible had they been the observations of his mother. They walked together day after day, sharing their observations of the natural world. They carved their names "on a large rock on the banks of Thirlmere, on their way north to Keswick", along with Coleridge, Mary Hutchinson, and others (Gittings & Manton, 1988, p. 102). These important and much valued activities had an emotional importance for them both, and gave each other a solid sense of being able to count on the love and concern of the other. They were each other's closest friend. However, what was different about their friendship was that they were also siblings. One of the qualities that makes sibling love strong and much valued is that it has its roots in the earliest years. Though Dorothy and William were separated for several years after the death of their mother, they had nevertheless shared, before the separation, an experience of being vulnerable children together. They knew each other better than anyone else. And this was to remain true in spite of William's marriage, or Dorothy's intense involvement with Coleridge. Dorothy and William's relationship was as "unalterably fixed" as was that of Freud (1900a, p. 483) and his nephew John. Unlike Freud, who had to look for substitutes for John, Dorothy and William could continue with their relationship throughout their lives.

I turn now to one of the most moving accounts of what I am calling "brotherly love". It is Anna Freud and Sophie Dann's (1951) account of six war orphaned children in their paper, "An experiment in group upbringing". The six war-orphaned children, three girls and three boys, were looked after and observed by Sophie Dann during 1945–1946, in a children's home that had been specially set up for them. It was called "Bulldogs Bank" and was in West Sussex. It was run for a year while adoptive homes were being found for them. There was a staff of four to help, including Sophie Dann's sister, Gertrud Dann. All six children were German–Jewish orphans. Four of the children had lost their parents at birth, and the other two at some time after birth. Their ages, at the time of coming into the home, ranged from three years to three years and ten months. They had survived their first few months of life being shuffled between refugee camps in Vienna, until finally they had been deported to the Polish concentration camp of Tereszin, by which time their ages were between six- and twelve-months old. None of them had ever known anything like "family life". They had never had enough food, few toys, and knew nothing about the outside world. The care they had known had been given by adult concentration camp victims who were necessarily impermanent. They were all approximately eighteen months behind in their developmental age when they arrived in England.

When they first arrived at "Bulldogs Bank", they were wild, noisy, broke the toys provided and were hostile to all the adults. They seemed to behave like wild animals, as they spat at and bit the grown ups, and the first six months of their stay was a turbulent time. The children's emotional moods would swing between extreme states of passivity or violence. But while they displayed this aggressive and inconsistent behaviour to the adults, within their tightly knit group they behaved with great concern for each other. They could not bear to be separated. One of the remarkable characteristics about this inseparable group was that there seemed to be no rigid leadership, but instead an extreme sensitiveness to each other's needs and feelings. There was also a complete lack of jealousy or rivalry within the group and they never had to be exhorted to share or take turns. They acted towards each other with generosity and pleasure, even when it came to meal times. They seemed to take more pleasure from sharing their food than in eating it themselves. It is true that they all had a difficult relationship with food, and tended to dislike new tastes, but even when it came to things that they loved, like sweets, they would share them. Their aggressiveness was expressed in verbal quarrels or in attacks against the adults.

After several months in "Bulldogs Bank", the children began to attach themselves to adults, and then their quarrels changed. They began to fight each other physically. There was one child whose behaviour had been more malicious and less cooperative within the group. This little girl had attached herself very passionately to an adult when she had been in the concentration camp. Once she had formed a new attachment to one of the carers, Gertrud Dann, her aggressive behaviour in the group disappeared.

Gradually, all the children began to form attachments to the adults, but not in the usual terms of dependency upon an adult. The children began to allow the adults into their group, but the adults were treated as if they were children. The children shared their toys and sweets with the adults, and in turn expected to share in the adult activities. The children's attachment to each other was never superseded by an attachment to an adult, with the exception of the little girl already mentioned. For the other five children, their primary attachment to each other was unwavering.

Freud and Dann concluded that the cooperative behaviour that these six children showed for each other was unheard of, and the direct result of the total absence of any adult to whom they could become attached. They were each other's most important loved object, and they preserved this love through all vicissitudes. The lack of any parental love in their internal world meant that the children were without the normal feelings of sibling rivalry. The one little girl who had known some sort of attachment to an adult, in the concentration camp, was the one who was the least integrated into the group. Freud and Dann seem to be suggesting that sibling rivalry and attachment to an adult, go hand in hand, or, that extreme sibling/peer attachment is linked to the absence of a parental object.

The theoretical background to their conclusion was essentially Freudian. They believed, like Freud, that siblings are always in rivalry for parental attention and love and that any positive feelings that might be observed between siblings are only a "reaction formation" to the desired relationship with the parent (Freud, 1916–1917). Therefore, for Freud and Dann, as for Freud himself, cooperative behaviour amongst children is always a reversal of hostility.

Freud and Dann not only thought that their observation supported Freud's theory on the essential nature of sibling relationships, they also thought it was a refutation of the Kleinian view that a disturbance in the mother–child relationship during the first years was the major cause of neurosis. They stressed that, although these children were difficult to manage, showed marked auto-erotic behaviour and, in one case, the beginnings of neurotic symptoms, they were not "deficient, delinquent or psychotic" (1951, p. 168). They concluded that these children survived psychologically intact and therefore the mother–child relationship could not be the necessary precondition for normal development in every case.

How can Freud and Dann's observation of these six children help us understand the concept of brotherly love? One response to the observation might be to say that we can learn nothing about peer group relationships and attachments from this study. These children were brought up in extraordinary circumstances, far from the normal sorts of attachments, and it would be misguided to extrapolate from their behaviour. For instance, there was no place for the individual child to be separate and alone, and therefore, it must have been a pathological group. Furthermore, the cooperation and altruism that they displayed were so exceptional that we can make no further inference. Perhaps, more importantly, it can be pointed out that these children were not siblings and therefore the crucial element of being displaced by a younger child was not part of their psychic experience.

I want to suggest another way of thinking about these six children and their relationships. Freud and Dann believed these children had survived psychologically intact, and were not deemed to be "deficient, delinquent or psychotic". How was this possible? What resources were they drawing on? How did they have the capacity to form a non-destructive social group? Have we got the right descriptions of child development if there can be children who survive psychologically intact, even though they have known none of the usual building bricks believed to be essential for psychological health?

I want to make it quite clear that I am not arguing that children should be brought up without parents, nor am I suggesting that children do not have murderous feelings towards each other, but I do believe that to see the parent–child relationship as the sole seat of health and pathology is to omit the importance of the sibling/peer relationship, most particularly when the parent/child relationship is absent or negative. It also elides the difference between what we learn in the nursery and what we learn at our parent's knee. Ideally we need both, and to make one relationship, the child/parent one, the sole seat of mental health is "a fundamental misreading of the family experience" (Sulloway, 1998, p. 146).

Bion (1961) and Foulkes (1964) have drawn our attention to the power of groups. Dalal (1998) has perspicaciously pointed out that the capacity to be separate, psychologically, which is the healthy outcome of parent/child love, is in conflict with the capacity to act altruistically in a group, which is the characteristic of sibling/peer relationships. He suggested that there are two distinct developmental strands that we all have to negotiate; the need to be separate from our parents, and the need to learn to cooperate with our siblings and peers. We have to move "from the singular I" to the many varieties of "us" (p. 226). What is so powerful about Freud and Dann's observation, was that, at the moment of the most unimaginable suffering, these children were able to continue to live and be creative. Dalal's point reinforces the suggestion that sibling/peer relationships may be nature's answer to a failed parent/child relationship.

With that thought in mind, I want to suggest that siblings and peers may be significantly important for the development of what Emde (1988) felicitously called the "we" ego. Emde was surveying the research on infant development to date and towards the end of the paper he suggests that we need a new concept of a "we" ego. That is to say, his own research led him to the "startling realization" that children, by the time they were three-years old, "had developed an executive sense of 'we', of the significant other being with them, which gave them increased sense of power and control". Indeed, he goes on to say that: "The child's developing sense of 'we' and the interpersonal world of shared meaning is now becoming an increasing focus of research attention among developmentalists and psycholinguists" (p. 36). It is true that his "startling realization" was linked to his work with mothers and children, and that the concept of a "we" ego referred to the capacity in the child to think of itself in relationship to its mother as a "we". However, Emde is also making a metapsychological point when he says:

> It is perhaps ironic that in our age, so preoccupied with narcissism and self, we are beginning to see a different aspect of psychology, a "we" psychology in addition to a "self" psychology. I draw attention to the fact that this represents a profound change in our world view. [p. 36]

In Chapter One, I had suggested that Mrs K moved between the wish to be the only child and the desire to be a member of the sibling clan. I want to end this chapter with a proposal that we borrow a concept from group psychology, whether it is Emde's "we" ego, or Dalal's, many varieties of "us", to help us understand how the six children that Freud and Dann (1951) observed had managed to survive. What they demonstrated was a capacity, that has not been sufficiently recognized in psychoanalytic thinking, to draw psychic nourishment and strength from an identification with the group; an identification that is not built upon Freud's "reaction-formation" of rivalry for parental attention (1921c, p. 120). There had been no parental attention. Therefore, these children drew upon an identification with the peer/sibling group for their psychic development. It is clearly shown in Freud and Dann's account that there is a tension between the one-to-one attachment of the child to the adult, and the children's attachment to the group, as I found with Mrs K. But this is a tightrope we all walk. If we take up Emde's concept of a "we" ego as well as an "ego" *tout court*, we might be able to redirect our thinking away from a narrow preoccupation with narcissism and self psychology, and question whether we have ignored a capacity that these six war-orphaned children demon-strated—a capacity for "brotherly love".[2] As Ruth, in Carson McCullers' novel, *The Member of the Wedding* (1982) commented at her brother's wedding: "You are the we of me" (p. 172).

Notes

1. The meaning of sisterhood associated with feminist discussions of the 70s and 80s are outside the scope of this chapter, but are usually linked with the idea of solidarity between women as opposed to competition between women for men. (I am indebted to Ann Scott for pointing out that I needed to make my use of "sisterhood" clear.)

2. Sarah Moskovitz (1983) followed up the six Bulldogs Bank children. She wanted to know: "what had become of these extraordinary children? What do they remember ...? How do they view ... their upbringing? And what do they have to teach us?" (p. 43). Two years after they left Bulldogs Bank, five of them had been adopted. Peter had been adopted, at four and a half, by an American couple. He had become a teacher. He had not married and he died of cancer soon after meeting Sarah Moskovitz. Miriam lived in London. She had been adopted when she was five. She was married with two children. She had had a difficult time in growing up, and felt she had given her adopted parents a hard time. She had not told her children about her past, and kept her

adoption hidden. Paul lived in America. He was the only one of the six children who had not been adopted, and had therefore been raised in Lingfield house, in the care of Alice Goldberger. When he was eighteen, his aunt and uncle, who themselves had survived several concentration camps, adopted him and took him to America. He had married unsuccessfully, and was still clearly quite disturbed. Ruth lived in London. She had been adopted, and was married with children. Her life was outwardly very successful. John was also adopted and lived in London, with his wife and two daughters. His background had been kept from him by his adopted parents, but he had found out quite a lot about his past once he had found himself a wife. He came across as a man in a lot of pain, but a man who was capable of love and loving. Finally, Leah, who lived in California. She had been adopted. She was the only one of the six who remembered the other children and wanted to know what had happened to them. She was married with four children. She went to a child guidance clinic, probably Anna Freud's, from seven until she left England at eighteen. Now she was agoraphobic.

CHAPTER EIGHT

The sibling experience

"The nature and quality of the human child's relations to
people of his own and the opposite sex have already been
laid down in the first six years of his life ... The people to
whom he is in this way fixed are his parents and brothers and
sisters"

Freud, 1914f, p. 243

I
n the last chapter, on brotherly love, I suggested that sibling/
peer relationships need to be brought into sharper focus in our
thinking about the development of the self. In this chapter, I
shall be looking at writers who share my view that relationships
between siblings and peers are to be distinguished from those
between parent and child and that they hold a particular and
important place in the inner world.

It may seem that the quotation above, from Freud's short paper,
"Some reflections on schoolboy psychology", is an acknowledgment
of the importance of sibling relationships. We have already seen
how, in 1900a, he had noted his early relationship with his nephew
John was "unalterably fixed" (p. 483) in his unconscious, and that

his way of relating to his contemporaries in later life was determined by this experience. However, my argument throughout this book is that Freud's belief in the importance of these early experiences with siblings and peers drops out of his clinical theory and practice and remains at the stage of intuitive insight. I have already suggested, in Chapter Two, that Freud's complicated family background may give some understanding of his emotional conflict surrounding early attachment to siblings and peers. I have also argued that Freud's discovery of the Oedipus complex contributed to the abandonment of the theoretical problem of sibling attachments.

Freud's reluctance to pursue more deeply the question of how early sibling/peer relationships "fix" later ones, has meant there has been a lack of interest in this idea, at both the level of theory and in clinical practice. We still consider these relationships to be unimportant. If you pick up any clinical paper on adult therapy today, it would be hard to find an account of sibling relationships and their impact upon the present circumstances. To give an example, I was sent a diagnostic assessment of a young woman by a medically qualified psychotherapist at one of the major teaching hospitals in London. The patient's relationship with her mother and her father was extensively explored and her pathology was attributed to the difficulties that she had with them. There was no mention of any siblings in the family, except for a cursory one line, "the patient had an incestuous relationship with a brother in adolescence". Further reference to the brother, or to the effect of the incest upon the presenting problem, was not made and their age differences were ignored. There is nothing exceptional about this assessment. This is the norm. Pathology has not been connected to sibling relationships, nor even to incestuous ones.

In the early eighties, at Yale University in the United States, an interest in sibling relationships and their effect upon emotional development was shown. The Yale University research group consisted of American Professors of Paediatrics, Psychiatrists, Psychoanalysts, and Lecturers, A. J. Solnit, A. Colonna, M. Kris, P. B. Neubauer, S. Provence, and S. Ritvo. They set up a longitudinal study on the development of pre-school siblings who were two years apart in age in order: "to study the mutual influences from year to year" (Neubauer, 1982, p. 122). Their findings were published in England in *The Psychoanalytic Study of the Child* in 1982 and 1983.

The basic assumption of this research group was that siblings and their relationships to each other were important and could affect emotional development. They challenged the centrality of Freud's Oedipus complex and set out to show that sibling relationships were not "second editions" of the original parental one (Colonna & Newman, 1983). They believed there could be other ways of seeing and thinking about siblings. They also challenged Freud's theory that the fundamental bedrock of the sibling relationship is one of rivalry.

It was observed that, though the birth of a sibling increased the aggressive drive of an elder child (Neubauer, 1982), if all goes well, the elder child learns how to manage better its aggressive drives. In other words, the birth of a sibling can be creative for the older child even though its ego development and defences are naturally affected. It was acknowledged that aggression was activated at the birth of the new baby, but it was suggested that rivalry and jealousy are not the fundamental bedrock of the sibling experience. They are just a part of the sibling experience.

This research group also suggested that when a child has a sibling it is faced with a different set of triangulations in both the pre-oedipal and the oedipal phase (Kris & Ritvo, 1983). Love and jealousy between siblings is different to the oedipal conflict between parents and children. A child who has negotiated sibling rivalry may be helped to manage oedipal frustration and conflict more easily. One reason for this is that a sibling rival is smaller than a parent. This literally lessens the size of the task that has to be negotiated, and gives the child encouragement for negotiating the larger task of facing the parent. Or as Kris and Ritvo (1983) put it: "the sibling may be ... more malleable than the parent in the child's efforts to seek adaptive resolutions to the oedipal conflict" (p. 322). This point has strong echoes of Klein's (1932) view that the fear of parents can be so strong that the Oedipus complex could not be resolved without the help of a sibling or peer as an "ally" (p. 118).

The belief that siblings help each other to negotiate oedipal conflict lead Kris and Ritvo (1983) to suggest that the choice of a marital partner is always influenced by the sibling relationship. We have already seen that Klein (1932) was also of the view that oedipal conflict may need the support of sibling love and that: "the existence of a secret complicity of this sort ... plays an essential part in every relationship of love, even, between grown-up people" (p. 224). I think this is a point that has been almost entirely neglected in our formulation of adult sexual desire. I have found it useful, when I am listening to the clatter that surrounds a collapsing marriage, to hold in mind a distinction between the sounds of a primitive nursery squabble that has not been resolved and a quarrel that holds the angry disappointment of a love for a parent, that has not been given up or resolved. We bring both the sibling self and the parent/child self to a marriage, and what often needs sorting out, in such circumstances, is the difference between: "This is mine!", meaning, "This is my toy, and I don't want to share it with you, because you have been so horrible to me", and, "This is mine!" meaning, "I must have this new beautiful person who has come into my life, for in this way I shall find fulfilment".

What I found so striking about the Yale Study Group was that it was my first encounter with a group of people who thought siblings and their relationships were important contributors to our emotional development and internal world. It is disappointing to discover that their work has not been taken up and developed. In 1994 Sharpe and Rosenblatt could still write:

> the nature of sibling relationships, in all their complex forms of love and hate, still remains more of a mystery than the passions and developmental vicissitudes of parent–child relationships. [p. 491]

One reason why their work has not been continued, may be linked to the criticism that this type of empirical observation is made by those whose work is concentrated on the psychoanalytic encounter.

André Green (2000) maintains that the art of psychoanalysis involves the gradual uncovering of unconscious fantasies via the blocks set up by resistance and defence. This slow discovery of unconscious desire has nothing to do with observation and empirical research. The unconscious can only be observed through the intimate understanding of the dream. He gives a description of what goes on in an analytical session. The patient freely associates and the analyst's attention is aroused by something that is said. (He calls it c.) Later on the patient mentions something quite different (m and n) and the analyst begins to put together c and m and n. Then, m and n and c become linked to further associations. He then goes on to say: "This entirely new set of connections gives birth to the repressed and the unconscious" (*ibid.*, p. 33). He concludes:

> We see here that reversal of meaning, which is coexistent with the intervention of the defences, mainly repression, totally escapes the possibility of being observed in any way other than the type of awareness stemming from the clinical situation. [p. 33–34]

Green believes psychoanalysis will not survive if it is diluted by the external and non-analytic inputs of infant observation, for it will be turned into a general psychology of human development. My question is, however, if psychoanalysis is not tethered by a general psychology of human development, where is it centred? Can psychoanalysis grow and change only if it can let in new ideas from within its own practice? Freud's theories changed and developed through his observations of his patients, as well as through the analysis of his own dreams. From Green's perspective, how can a conceptual mistake, or for that matter, a factual mistake be approached?

Green's idea, that the analytic encounter needs preserving from the contamination of infant observation and the psychology of human development, shows up an epistemological divide within psychoanalytic theory. What is the nature of psychoanalytic knowledge? How do we gain knowledge of it? The most common battle ground is laid out between the "interpsychic" and the "intrapsychic". Each side eyes the other with suspicion, while trying to claim the moral high ground. I believe psychoanalytic theory is weakened if it is not informed by observations that come from outside the pathological. The Yale Study Group and many others observing infants *in statu nascendi* have brought about a radical alteration in the psychoanalytic perspective. The day-to-day observation of the unfolding of children's relationships with each other has helped to reveal that the Cain complex is not the whole story. Siblings can engage in cooperative play as much as aggressive attack and they can become deeply attached to each other. But because we have tended to ignore the importance of these relationships, we have hardly begun to think about, for instance, the experience of loss a younger sibling may feel when an older sibling goes off to school (Leitchman, 1985).

Piontelli (1989, 1992) has observed, through scans, twins *in utero* and has drawn attention to the possibility that twins are making relationships with each other before they are born. She has observed twins who seem be actively hostile to each other and continue to reject each other after birth. There have been others who have developed a loving and playful relationship in the womb. Piontelli's work raises a more general question about how sibling relationships are formed. The six war-orphaned children from Theresienstadt, described in Chapter Seven, made me wonder if our description of infant development is too narrow. These children seemed to have made loving and cooperative relationships amongst themselves with the total absence of parental figures. Where does that capacity come from? What is happening in the internal world if we can observe infants *in utero* making relationships that affect the rest of their lives?

The philosophical belief, that empirical research contaminates the analytic process, as outlined by such theorists as Green, has meant we have little empirical or theoretical idea about sibling position and its effect upon the developing psyche. Freud wrote: "The position of a child in the family order is a factor of extreme importance in determining the shape of his later life" (1916d, p. 334). However, I have failed to find any clinical examples in Freud where the sibling position is credited with significance. For instance in "The Wolfman", the potential significance of his place in the family is brushed aside by Freud's insistence that his neurosis was the result of the trauma of witnessing the primal scene. Sibling position becomes further weakened as an idea by an implicit assumption in Freud, despite the statement from him above, that the sibling experience must be the same whatever place the child may have within the family. For him all children are rivals for parental attention. The Yale University researchers, and others (Bank & Kahn, 1982; Dunn & Kendrick, 1982; Graham, 1988), suggest it is an epistemological error to assume that the more conflictual feelings of the eldest sibling *are* the sibling experience. We have seen George Eliot's perceptive illustration of Maggie and Tom's feelings for each other. She understood the dynamic difference between an older child's feelings towards a younger sibling, and the younger sibling's feelings towards the older child. An eldest child may feel robbed of his unique position in the family when the next sibling is born. The next sibling, however, will never have known a world without siblings and will never have had the experience of being the only pebble on the beach, as it were. It is simply incorrect to extrapolate from the possible experience of the eldest child to all subsequent children. Sharpe and Rosenblatt (1994) are sensitive to the difference that sibling order may have upon emotional development and suggest there will be a tendency for the eldest child to have a relationship of hostility towards a younger sibling in the beginning, and a positive attachment will only develop later. By contrast, the younger sibling is, "rarely being motivated by envy or anger toward the older sibling" (p. 517) in the beginning. It is true that when Freud came to discussing the birth of a sibling for a little girl, he claimed it could be a good thing, for it could arouse her curiosity and wish for a baby. It is interesting that he does not seem to have subscribed to the corollary that the birth of a sibling could be creative for a boy.

One idea that has emerged from the Yale Symposium is that the role of identification with a sibling plays an important part in psychic development. Siblings can, for instance, form strong attachments to each other before the age of six months and, at times, understand each other better than a parent (Leichtman, 1985; Neubauer, 1983). It has been observed that they smile more at each other than at parents or other adults (Parens, 1988). A mutual identification can also be seen in shared acts of anger or wickedness against the adults. Sibling identification can take different forms, and perhaps the most powerful is the "secret complicity" of the erotic attachment between siblings that Klein (1932) described.

Agger (1988) robustly stated:

> Most analysts see sibling love as defensive and as an oedipal derivative. Clinical and personal experience leads me to wonder if we have not underestimated the strength and durability of this separate reservoir of love objects. [p. 27]

She believes ego development and character is affected and altered by sibling relationships, positively and negatively, and reiterates the idea, already discussed by Klein and the Yale Researchers, that sibling relationships can ease oedipal conflict with parents. She does not believe sibling conflict is the norm, but that it is most often the result of unresolved conflict that the parents are still having with their own siblings. As I stated in my introduction, this is an important area of study that I have not touched upon.

Agger believes that sibling relationships can be manifold; if they are very negative, they can result in emotional and intellectual inhibition. Sibling love and support can lead to emotional and intellectual stability, especially if the parents are grossly negligent, as in the example she cites of the Sitwell family The failure of psychoanalytic theory to conceptualize the importance of siblings led her to question whether the concept of the Oedipus complex had served a neurotic need in Freud. As we saw in Chapter Three, Agger is not alone in thinking that Freud had been unable to deal with the death of his brother, Julius, the birth of his sister, Anna, or the ambivalent passion for his nephew, John. But, what distinguishes Agger's view from others, is her belief that murderous and incestuous wishes towards siblings can be felt to be more threatening than those towards parents. For instance, if a sibling dies, the guilt may be overwhelming. Equally, incestuous wishes, just because they can be more easily enacted, may be felt to be too much to manage. Therefore the Oedipus complex serves a defensive purpose. Lesser (1978) had suggested that the psychoanalytic practice of expecting the patient to lie on the couch, puts the psychoanalyst in the position of an authority figure, encourages the oedipal drama and obscures possible sibling relationships, though she does not go so far as to state that the Oedipus complex is a defence against the more powerful sibling relationship.

Mitchell (2000), in her recent book on siblings, comes close to the idea of re-centring sibling relationships and the Oedipus complex. She seems to be agreeing with Agger when she writes:

> Freud's (and all subsequent psychoanalytic) emphasis on the intergenerational Oedipus complex indicates a massive repression of the significance of all the love and hate of sibling relationship and their heirs in marital affinity and friendships. [p. 77]

However, Mitchell is a committed "classical" Freudian psychoanalyst in the sense that she believes in Freud's drive theory and the concept of the death instinct, so her task of re-centring sibling relationships alongside the Oedipus complex is more subtle and complicated.

Mitchell accepts Freud's own characterization of the Oedipus complex as the "shibboleth that distinguishes the adherents of psychoanalysis from its opponents" (Freud, 1905d, p. 226n), yet she also asserts that, "Freud unconsciously wanted to avoid the significance of ... [sibling relationships] which would have placed in jeopardy his emerging Oedipus complex" (Mitchell, 2000, p. 106). This unconscious conflict in Freud's thinking creates a difficulty in Mitchell's theory as well. On the one hand, she accepts that what distinguishes psychoanalysis is the shibboleth of the Oedipus complex. On the other hand, she argues that the Oedipus complex avoids or represses sibling relationships. Mitchell suggests the conflict could be overcome if psychoanalysis began to incorporate ideas from anthropology and evolutionary psychology. In this way, psychoanalysis could begin to restructure its theory and practice and allow a place for the affiliations of siblings in understanding adult relationships. I have already stated my belief that psycho-analysis needs to be open to knowledge that is being gained in other areas of human development, and so I am sympathetic to Mitchell's suggestion. However, Mitchell does not go into the specific contributions that evolutionary psychology might make, for instance, and instead seems to rely on an implicit thesis taken from evolutionary theory. This theory suggests that, in terms of survival, it makes sense to murder your siblings but not your mother or father (Sulloway, 1998). In Mitchell's hands this becomes: "When the child is replaced by the sibling, initially this feels like annihilation; *'murder' is the reaction of the fittest*" (p. 335, my italics).[1] This idea, that the wish to murder gets into the psyche at the birth of a sibling, is what propels her argument to:

> invert accepted psychoanalytic ordering, which leads from the Oedipus complex on to the siblings, and suggest instead that it is the initial awareness of the presence of the siblings which produces a catastrophic psychosocial situation of displacement. This triggers in turn a regression to the earlier parental relationships *which were without their psychic implications until this moment*. [p. 22, my italics]

The notion that the earlier parental relationships "were without psychic implications" before the birth of sibling is hard to understand. What about the only child? I think Mitchell's argument gets into difficulty, because she is trying to accommodate her deeply held Freudian beliefs with some of the more radical ideas from anthropology and evolutionary psychology. In the end, sibling relationships and their significance within the psyche has not shifted. We are still left with the Freudian straitjacket of an *essentialist* theory about sibling hostility. Murder is in the air, but now it is no longer the wish to murder the parent of the opposite sex, it is to murder the sibling who threatens to displace one. Siblings re-enter the stage with a far more powerful psychic role to play, but they are still hated and, on Mitchell's account, our deepest wish must be to get rid of them.

I have argued, throughout the book, that I believe Freud's position on siblings is too narrow. I am suggesting that what starts out as a more radical view returns Mitchell to a similar Freudian position. I think it is a mistake to leave out the possibility that a child with a sibling can begin to gain some new control in the world. Kissing, biting, hitting, holding, are activities that can now become more powerful and effective when directed towards a sibling. The child's world is no longer peopled with giants. The cupboard under the stairs can become a sanctuary, a house of one's own to be shared with another person who is equally small. Identification with parental figures takes on a new meaning when there are brothers and sisters with whom to play "mothers and fathers".

Mitchell's belief in the catastrophic nature of the birth of a sibling means that her theory leaves out the possibility that these new "lateral" (p. 40) relationships can open up the world in a new and positive way. There is a further difficulty in her characterization of sibling relationships. She criticizes Freud, Lacan, and Winnicott for their neglect of siblings on the strength that she believes that peers and siblings can act as "mirrors" for each other. An "older child can surely also act as (an) appropriate container ... for the still uncoordinated movements of the infant" (p. 106) she says. But what are older siblings containing for the younger child? Mitchell says that an older child can be a "mirror" and give "an identification" (p. 107) to another child, but, she concludes, it is a false mirror or identification. She takes the case of Freud's (1905e) Dora and her brother Otto, and suggests that when Dora "look(ed) ... in the mirror of her brother she would have seen her unitary self" (*ibid.*). But, Mitchell goes on to assert, that mirror gave Dora a false belief that she was the same as Otto, therefore in "having an older brother, Dora is *exiled* from her boy-like self just as effectively as she would have been had she had a younger sibling" (*ibid.*).

As with Mitchell's argument that the wish to murder gets into the psyche with the arrival of a sibling, I find the idea that sibling identification is a distortion puts siblings back into a place in the inner world where their impact is yet again reduced to what is negative and destructive. We need to find a theoretical place for siblings which will accommodate the complexity of our emotions towards them and which will resist the tendency to reduce them to hated, unwanted, and distorting figures to our developing selves.

Note

1. Such a view is explicitly stated by Sulloway in his book *Born to Rebel* (1998). His argument rests upon the Darwinian idea that we are all trying to maximize our fitness, and in the case of siblings, we are trying to gain the most parental love and attention. The way in which siblings compete for these scarce resources he call "sibling strategies" (p. 119). For instance, the eldest child will devise ways in which to be different from his younger siblings in order to gain most attention. Sulloway studied more than a thousand biographies and came to the conclusion that birth order was the crucial factor in determining character and fate. Eldest children tend to be conservative, for in this way they gain most parental approval. Younger children tend to be rebels for they realize that, in order to get as much attention as possible, they are most likely to succeed by making as much noise as possible, notably by challenging parental norms. Sulloway's argument seems to support the Freudian thesis of the essential rivalry of siblings and the Mitchell thesis that we wish to murder our siblings. There are, however, important differences in their two arguments. Sulloway gives priority to biology and the need to survive, whereas Mitchell gives primacy to the libidinal, and therefore the need to reproduce. Mitchell believes in the Oedipus complex, whereas Sulloway believes that, "competition between siblings is more fundamental even than competition for mates" (p. 354). Though there are distinct differences between the Freudian/ Mitchell theatre of the mind and the Sulloway one, the combined arguments of Mitchell and Sulloway reinstate the Freudian thesis that siblings wish (Mitchell), or need (Sulloway) to get rid of each other.

CHAPTER NINE

Conclusion

"What do we know ourselves, how do we remember, and what is it we find in the end?"

Sebald, 2001, p. 287

The central question I have been asking throughout this book is, why have siblings been relegated to a peripheral place in the psychoanalytic inner world? One answer to the question lies in the prominent position that psychoanalytic theory has placed upon Freud's Oedipus complex. As I pursued the question further, I became aware of the personal way in which siblings were thought about, by such theorists as Freud and Klein. This led me to suggest that the Freudian proposal, of the universality of the rivalrous nature of sibling relationships, should be tempered with the idea that psychoanalysis might be conceived of as the theorization of autobiography.

I ended the last chapter with the argument that if we believe that the primary emotion siblings have towards each other is one of murderous wishes, we are forced into thinking that any other emotions they might have towards each other are displaced or "second editions" (Colonna & Newman, 1983). Mitchell's *Mad Men & Medusa* (2000) re-addresses the powerful impact that siblings have upon emotional development, but I find her view is too restricting. I argued that her deeply held Freudian beliefs lead her back to the *essentialist* position, in which siblings are again reduced to hated rivals. I agree that the birth of a sibling can herald a catastrophic and murderous reaction, but it does not follow that the intrinsic nature of sibling relationships is predicated upon displacement. For instance, a second child comes into a very different world to a first child. In the examples of George Eliot, Melanie Klein, the war-orphaned children from Theresienstadt, and my work with some of my patients, they express loving feelings towards their siblings/peers, and these feelings play a significant part in the structure of the psyche.

Sibling love has been ignored in the psychoanalytic literature, and we get only fleeting glimpses of its power in the research work of the Yale University, Bank and Kahn (1982), Volkan and Ast (1997), and Melanie Klein (1932). We may not be prepared to go along with Klein's idea that sexual relations between siblings can facilitate later heterosexual development, but this view does challenge the "classical" psychoanalytic assumption that sibling/peer relationships are essentially held in the quicksand of rivalry for parental love. Freud intuitively toyed with such a competing theory of mind. For instance, in his paper on Jensen's *Gradiva* which I summarized in a note in Chapter Four, he seems to suggest that relationships amongst children can determine later choices of sexual partners. However, these insights are either rejected or stay as footnotes to the body of his work. We need to consider whether the resolution of our sexual desires for our parents is the only path by which sexual maturity is achieved. I think we should take seriously the idea that successful adult sexual attachment may involve the "secret complicity" of sibling sexual attachment. A more thorough study of this area of our emotional life needs to be made, and I have merely hinted at its importance.

This leads into another area that still awaits much fuller investigation, namely the role of sibling identification within the psyche. Mitchell's belief is that sibling identification is a distorting mirror. In the work of Neubauer (1983), Leitchman (1985), and Parens (1988) there is a more positive picture of sibling identification.

Siblings smile at each other more, intuitively pick up the feelings of the other sibling more quickly, and when they are separated they can experience intense feelings of loss. One way of conceptualizing sibling/peer identification might be to say it gives rise to or strengthens a "we" ego. This is a concept that is borrowed from Emde's (1988) observations of mother/infant interaction. He suggested that a forgotten area of emotional development was the subtle way in which the child, by the age of three, becomes able to distinguish between itself, as an I, and itself with another, as a "we". This idea of a "we" ego links naturally to the work of group analysis where more attention is given to the role of siblings within group dynamics. Dalal (1998) distinguishes between the emotional effects that are created between parents and children, and the many varieties of "us" that we experience with our siblings/peers. One way of thinking about the role of sibling identification may be to say that it helps the development of a "we" ego, which allows us to imagine "the many varieties of us".

I have found the idea of "oedipal sibling triangles" (Sharpe & Rosenblatt, 1994) useful in thinking about intractable sibling difficulties. I did not have the conceptual tools to think in this way with Mr Y or Mr T, but my work with Mrs Z began to give me some idea of the difference between parental oedipal triangles and sibling oedipal triangles. Mrs Z could express a longing to be the only child with her parents, but at the same time she knew this position excluded her from the sibling clan that she enjoyed. She wanted both positions and did not know how to encompass them. Were they incompatible? Had there been a failure of integration? Or did she have to accept that both places required renouncement or exclusion? I do not feel able to answer those questions satisfactorily, but I do think that Mrs Z's conflict, between the wish to be a member of the sibling clan and to be the only child, needs further clarification and representation.

It became clear to me that an excessively strong sibling relationship and parental inattention or neglect go hand in hand. This idea was confirmed when I thought about the reasons for sibling incest. The case of Byron and his half-sister, Augusta, and the intuitive insights of such writers as Byatt (1992) and Dunmore (1996), would seem to confirm this point of view. In the cases of Mrs K and Mr T, I came to understand that their extremely punitive superego was linked to sibling cruelty. Sibling cruelty seems to eat into the psyche with a ferocity that is commensurate with the actual experience and gives a different twist to the harsh superego. For instance, with Mrs K and Mr T, they had fantasies of a harsh, unyielding, punishing world in which there was an almost total absence of hope that this situation could be ameliorated, except in unthinkably murderous fantasies of revenge. I link this inner world to the lengthy time of caring they had in the hands of older siblings. I believe these older siblings did not bring more moderate or modulating fantasies that come with maturity and parental concerns, and that these less modulated fantasies were the ones that Mrs K and Mr T had internalized. This is an area that remains largely unexplored, for most clinical material links a harsh superego to an introjected parental figure. I believe that, if we begin to take notice of the effects of the sibling relationship upon the developing psyche, a distinction between introjected parents and introjected siblings will give us a more rounded picture of the superego.

I have found a harsh sibling superego much more difficult to shift. This experience does not lead me to believe in the death instinct, as an explanation for the obduracy of this sadomasochistic position. I find it sufficient to think that these people have had their egos crushed and their trust in the goodness of the world has been rent apart.

A question that has puzzled me and links back to sibling identification, is whether sibling relationships are ever given up. We have an analytic theory that suggests there is an impulse to resolve oedipal conflict and become separate from our parents. We also believe that without this resolution our sexual life is diminished. Is there a similar impulse or need to grow up and away from our siblings? If sibling love plays a part in our sexual maturity, what happens when sibling love goes wrong? Can an over intense relationship with a sibling inhibit our sexual development? I have suggested that a difference can be heard between a marriage that is foundering upon an intense nursery squabble and one that has hit upon parental oedipal conflict, though of course the two are intermingled. A marriage that is foundering on a nursery quarrel may prove to be more difficult to resolve, for there is more narcissistic humiliation involved in relinquishing a sibling battle (Sharpe & Rosenblatt, 1994).

The failure to think about sibling identification may account for the absence of the concept of a sibling transference in the psychoanalytic literature. I have suggested that a therapy may founder on an undiagnosed sibling transference, like a marriage that is breaking down over a nursery quarrel. To encounter the raw passions of the nursery within a therapy can be an alarming experience. I know that when I encounter such a situation I have to struggle not to retreat to the safer territory of a parent dealing with a difficult child. Agger (1988) was one of the first clinicians to give expression to these fears. She discovered a reluctance within herself to think about sibling dynamics for they can give rise in the therapist to, "counter-transference issues, inhibitions and anxiety regarding competition and incest" (*ibid.*). I have found that the sibling transference feels much less safe. It can be more intense and erotic, as I discovered with Mr Y. At other times it seems more devious, quixotic and "noisy", as I realized with Mr T. With the latter, I could have sessions in which I seemed to be racing around in bewildering chaos, as though his words and associations were the embodiment of a small child trying to make sense of the myriad sibling affiliations that faced him each day. I could feel quite exhausted as I metaphorically raced around after him. If it is true that sibling relationships are not given up in the same way as parent/child ones, there may be a more intuitive anxiety about the ending of an analysis if the sibling transference is encountered. Could this offer a partial explanation for the dearth of clinical papers?

In my Introduction, I suggested that autobiography plays an invaluable part in psychoanalytic theory. Such a thought came about through my reading of Freud and Klein on siblings. But it is also true that I have drawn upon the memory and experience I had as a child with my siblings. It seems quite clear to me that the emotional impact my parents have had upon me cannot be superimposed upon the effect of the nursery life I experienced with my siblings. If I try to do so I blur a vital distinction that is part of my inner world. My childhood was held in the form that my parents created. The outward form was composed of such things as the house they bought, the number of children they had, the bedrooms we slept in, the people that helped in our upbringing. It also was made up of the emotional contours that my parents brought to the family life they created; their dreams, their anxieties and the social milieu they found themselves in, as well as their responses to us and our responses to them. All this has deeply affected my emotional life and the way I am in the world. My dependency and emotional vulnerability were uniquely contained by them, and in my inner fantasies no brother or sister could be confused with the awesome awareness of the bounteous creativity of parental figures, whose absence or withdrawal could challenge my ongoing belief in the goodness of the world. However, I feel, with equal passion, that the experience I had in the nursery with my siblings forms a crucial structure to my emotional world. I never laughed with my parents as I did with my siblings. I never played the same games with them. Sharing with my siblings was not an empty exhortation to "do as you'd be done by"; it became the foundation of games that could continue creatively (or not, as was so often the case). I never wished my parents to be gone forever, with the same and intense passionate conviction as I did when I quarrelled with a brother or sister. The daily contact with my siblings was far more extensive than with my parents. We shared bedrooms, took baths together, went for walks, and the same books nurtured our imagination. I do not want to give the impression that as a result of our shared nursery life we would give identical expression to our childhood experiences. Our emotional and imaginative capacities made what they could out of these experiences and they are very different. I learned some things at my mother's knee, and I learned other things with my siblings. These other things that I learned with my siblings, and then my peers, are an important part of who I am today. The jealous uprush I can feel when overlooked or ignored by my peers, or the delight in a group activity, can, in many cases, be associated to sibling experiences, and I believe I need to be sensitively aware of these possibilities, both in myself and in the daily exploration of my analytic work.

In conclusion, I return to Freud. I am sure he was intuitively right when he described the importance that his nephew, John, had upon all later transactions with his contemporaries. What I have attempted to show is that his intuitive insight needs to be brought into our psychoanalytic theories, and we need to explore more thoroughly the way this "passionate store" (Eliot, 1896, p. 213) can become "unalterably fixed" (Freud, 1900a, p. 483) in our unconscious minds.

It is to George Eliot (1992) I wish to turn for the last word on the significance of sibling relationships. I believe she spoke for more than Tom in *The Mill on the Floss*, when she had him say at the end of the novel that: "it came with so overpowering a force—it was such a new revelation to his spirit, of the depths of life that had lain beyond his vision" (p. 597).

REFERENCES

Abraham, H. C. (1950). Twin relationship and womb fantasies in a case of anxiety hysteria. *International Journal of Psychoanalysis, 34*: 219–227.

Agger, E. M. (1988). Psychoanalytic perspectives on sibling relationships. *Psychoanalytic Inquiry, 8*: 3–30.

Anzieu, D. (1986). *Freud's Self-Analysis*. London: Hogarth Press & The Institute of Psychoanalysis.

Ascherman, L. I., & Safier, E. J. (1990). Sibling incest: a consequence of individual and family dysfunction. *Bulletin of Menninger Clinic, 54*: 311–322.

Bank, S. P., & Kahn, M. D. (1980). Freudian siblings. *Psychoanalytic Review, 67*: 493–504.

Bank, S. P., & Kahn, M. D. (1997). *The Sibling Bond*. New York: Basic Books.

Bion, W. R. (1961). *Experience in Groups*. London: Tavistock/Routledge

Bonaparte, M. (1953). *Female Sexuality*. New York: International University Press.

Bowlby, J. (1980). *Attachment & Loss. Loss, Sadness and Depression. Volume 3*. Harmondsworth: Penguin.

Britton, R. (1998). *Belief and Imagination*, New Library of Psychoanalysis 31. London: Routledge.

Britton, R. (2002). Second thoughts on narcissism. (Talk given at the London Centre for Psychotherapy.)

Burlingham, D. T. (1945). The fantasy of having a twin. *Psychoanalytic Study of the Child*, 1: 205–210.

Burlingham, D. T. (1951). *Twins. A Study of Three Pairs of Twins*. New York: International Universities Press.

Byatt, A. S. (1992). *Angels & Insects*. London: Vintage.

Coles, P. (1975). Vico; the middle way. Unpublished MA thesis. Kent University.

Coles, P. (1998). The Children in the Apple Tree. *Australian Journal of Psychotherapy*, 1 & 2: 10–33.

Colonna, A. B., & Newman, L. M. (1983). The psychoanalytic literature on siblings. *Psychoanalytic Study of the Child*, 38: 285–309.

Conradi, P. J. (2001). *Iris Murdoch. A Life*. London: HarperCollins.

Dalal, F. (1998). *Taking the Group Seriously*. London: Jessica Kingsley.

Darbishire, H. (Ed.) (1958). *The Journals of Dorothy Wordsworth*. London: Oxford University Press.

Dunmore, H. (1996). *A Spell of Winter*. Harmondsworth: Penguin Books.

Dunn, J., & Kendrick, C. (1982). *Siblings; Love, Envy & Understanding*. Cambridge, Mass.: Harvard University Press.

Eliot, G. (1860). *The Mill on the Floss*. UK: Random House Ltd, 1992.

Eliot, G. (1896). *The Legend of Jubal and Other Poems*. Berlin: Albert Cohn.

Ellenberger, H. F. (1970). *The Discovery of the Unconscious: The History and Evolution of Dynamic Psychiatry*. New York: Basic Books.

Emde, R. N. (1988). Development terminable & interminable. 1. Innate motivational factors from infancy. *International Journal of Psychoanalysis*, 69(1): 23–42.

Farmer, P. (2000). *Sisters. An Anthology*. London: Penguin Books.

Finkelhor, D. (1980). Sex among siblings: a survey on prevalence, variety & its effects. *Archives of Sexual Behaviour*, 9: 171–194.

Fliess, R. (1956). *Erogeneity and Libido*. New York: International Universities Press.

Ford, J. (1633). "'Tis Pity She's a Whore". In: *Webster & Ford. Selected Plays*. London: Everyman.

Foulkes, S. H. (1964). *Therapeutic Group Analysis*. George Allen & Unwin Ltd.

Freud, A., & Dann, S. (1951). An experiment in upbringing. *Psychoanalytic Study of the Child*, 6: 127–168.

Freud, S. (1896c). *The Aetiology of the Neuroses. S.E., 3*.

Freud, S. (1899a). *Screen Memories. S.E., 3*.

Freud, S. (1900a). *Interpretation of Dreams. S.E., 4–5.*

Freud, S. (1905d). Three essays on sexuality. *S.E., 7.*

Freud, S. (1905e). Fragment of an analysis of a case of hysteria. *S.E., 7.*

Freud, S. (1909b). Analysis of a phobia in a five-year-old-boy. *S.E., 10.*

Freud, S. (1909d). *Notes upon a Case of Obsessional Neurosis. S.E., 10.*

Freud, S. (1907a). Delusion and dreams in Jensen's *Gradiva. S.E., 9.*

Freud, S. (1910a). Five lectures on psycho-analysis. *S.E., 11.*

Freud, S. (1912–1913). *Totem and Taboo. S.E., 13.*

Freud, S. (1914f). Some reflections on schoolboy psychology. *S.E., 13.*

Freud, S. (1915c). *Instincts and their Vicissitudes. S.E., 14.*

Freud, S. (1916–1917). Introductory lectures on psycho-analysis. *S.E., 15–16.*

Freud, S. (1916d). Some character-types met with in psycho-analytic work. *S.E., 14.*

Freud, S. (1918b). From the history of an infantile neurosis. *S.E., 17.*

Freud, S. (1921c). Group psychology and the analysis of the ego. *S.E., 18.*

Freud, S. (1925d). An autobiographical study. *S.E., 20.*

Freud, S. (1931b). Female sexuality. *S.E., 21.*

Freud, S. (1935a). *Postscript to an Autobiographical Study. S.E., 20.*

Freud, S. (1936). Draft of a letter to Thomas Mann in Fliess, R. (1956).

Freud, S. (1939a). *Moses and Monotheism. S.E., 23.*

Gay, P. (1988). *Freud. A Life for our Times.* London: J. M. Dent & Sons Ltd.

Gittings, R., & Manton, J. (1988). *Dorothy Wordsworth.* Oxford: O.U.P.

Glenn, J. (1966). Opposite sex twins. *Journal of American Psychoanalytic Association, 14:* 627–657.

Graham, I. (1988). The sibling object and its transferences. Alternate organisers of the middle field. *Psychoanalytic Inquiry, 8:* 88–107.

Graves, R. (1955). *Greek Myths. Volumes 1 2.* Penguin.

Graves, R., & Patai, H. (1966). *Hebrew Myths.* New York: McGraw Hill.

Green, A., & Stern, D. (2000). Clinical observational psychoanalytic research. Roots of controversy. In: Sandler, Sandler & Davies (Eds.), *Psychoanalytic Monographs, 5.* London & New York: Karnac Books.

Grosskurth, P. (1985). *Melanie Klein. Her World and Her Work.* London: Maresfield Library.

Grosskurth, P. (1991). *The Secret Ring. Freud's Inner Circle & The Politics of Psychoanalysis.* London: Jonathen Cape.

Grosskurth, P. (1997). *Byron. The Flawed Angel.* London: Hodder & Stoughton

Gubrich-Simitis, I. (2002). How Freud revised *The Interpretation of Dreams*: conflicts around the subjective origins of the book of the century. *Psychoanalysis and History, 4(2):* 111–127.

Harris, J. R. (1999). *The Nuture Assumption*. London: Bloomsbury.

Harrison, G. B. (1955). *The Elizabethan Journals*. London: Routledge & Kegan Paul.

Holmes, J. (1993). *John Bowlby & Attachment Theory*. London: Routledge.

Johnston, J. (1999). *The Invisible Worm*. Review. London: Headline Book.

Jones, E. (1953). *Sigmund Freud: A Life & Work, 3 Vols*. London: Hogarth Press.

Klein, M. (1926). The psychological principles of early analysis. In: *Love, Guilt & Reparation & Other Works*. (a) Delta Book, 1975. New York: Dell.

Klein, M. (1927). Criminal tendencies in normal children. (*ibid.*).

Klein, M. (1932). *The Psychoanalysis of Children*. (b) Delta Book, 1975. New York: Dell.

Klein, M. (1940). Mourning and its relation to manic depressive states. In: *Envy & Gratitude*. (c) Delta Book, 1975. New York: Dell.

Kris, M., & Ritvo, S. (1983). Parents and siblings. Their mutual influences. *Psychoanalytic Study of the Child, 38*: 311–324.

Laplanche, J. (1989). *New Foundations for Psychoanalysis*. Basil Blackwell Ltd.

Laplanche, J. (1999). *The Unconscious and the Id*. Rebus Press.

Leitchman, M. (1985). The influence of an older sibling on the separation–individuation process. *Psychoanalytic Study of the Child, 40*: 111–161.

Lesser, R. (1978). Sibling transference and countertransference. *Journal of Academic Psychoanalysis, 6*: 37–48.

Loredo, C. M. (1982). *Sibling incest*. In: S. M. Egroi (Ed.), *Handbook of Clinical Intervention in Child Sexual Abuse*. M.A.: D. C. Heath/ Lexington Books.

Luzes, P. (1990). Fact and fantasy in brother–sister incest. *International Review of Psychoanalysis, 17*(1): 97–113.

Mahony, P. J. (1984). *Cries of the Wolfman*. New York: International Universities Press.

Mann, T. (1951). *The Holy Sinner*. London: Penguin Books.

Martineau, H. (1877). *Autobiography. Volume 1*. London: Smith & Elder.

Masson, J. M. (1985). *The Complete Letters of Sigmund Freud to Wilhelm Fliess, 1887–1904*. Massachusetts, London: Harvard University Press.

McCullers, C. (1982). *The Member of the Wedding*. Harmondsworth: Penguin Books.

Mitchell, J. (2000). *Mad Men & Medusa. Reclaiming Hysteria and the Effect of Sibling Relations on the Human Condition*. Penguin Press: Allen Lane.

Mitchell, S. A. (1988). *Relational Concepts in Psychoanalysis*. Hillside, NJ: Analytic Press.

Moskovitz, S. (1983). *Love Despite Hate*. New York: Schocken Books.

Musil, R. (1930–1932). *The Man Without Qualities*. London: Picador.

Nabokov, V. (1971). *Ada*. Harmondsworth: Penguin Books.

Nagera, H. (1969). The imaginary companion. *Psychoanalytic Study of the Child*, 24: 165–196.

Nakashima, I. A., & Zakus, G. (1979). Incestuous families. *Pediatric Annals*, 8: 300–308.

Neubauer, P. B. (1982). Rivalry, envy and jealousy. *Psychoanalytic Study of The Child*, 37: 121–142.

Neubauer, P. B. (1983). The importance of the sibling experience. *Psycho-Analytic Study of The Child*, 38: 325–336.

NSPCC (2000). *Child Maltreatment in the United Kingdom. A Study of the Prevalence of Child Abuse and Neglect*. London: NSPCC.

Obholzer, K. (1982). *The Wolfman 60 Years Later. Conversations with Freud's Controversial Patient*. Routledge & Kegan Paul.

Parens, H. (1988). Siblings in early childhood; some direct observational findings. *Psychoanalytic Inquiry*, 8: 31–50.

Piontelli, A. (1989). Twins before and after birth. *International Review of Books*, 16(4): 413–426.

Piontelli, A. (1992). *From Fetus to Child*. London, New York: Tavistock/Routledge.

Prierl, B. (2002). Who killed Laius? On Sophocles' enigmatic message. *International Journal of Psychoanalysis*, 83(2): 433–443.

Rank, O. (1914). The double. In: *The Double, a Psychoanalytic Study*. London: Karnac Books, 1989.

Raphael-Leff, J. (1990). If Oedipus was an Egyptian. *International Review of Psycho-Analysis*, 17(3): 309–337.

Redinger, R. V. (1976). *George Eliot. The Emergent Self*. London, Sydney, Toronto: The Bodley Head.

Reich, A. (1932). *Analysis of a Case of Brother–Sister Incest. Psychoanalytic Contributions* (pp. 1–22). New York: International University Press, 1973.

Riemer, S. (1940). A research note on incest. *American Journal of Sociology*, 45: 554–565.

Schlesinger, K. (1969). In: *A Psychoanalytic View of the Family: A Study of Family Member Interactions* [A Symposium]. J. Lindon (Ed.), *Psychoanalytic Forum*, 3 (pp. 11–65). New York: International Universities Press.

Schwartz, J. (1999). *Cassandra's Daughter. A History of Psychoanalysis in Europe and America.* Allen Lane: The Penguin Press.

Sebald, W. G. (2001). *Austerlitz.* London: Hamish Hamilton.

Sharpe, S. A., & Rosenblatt, A. D. (1994). Oedipal sibling triangles. *Journal of American Psychoanalysis Association, 42*: 491–523.

Shaw, B. (1948). *Man & Superman* (Act II, p. 99). Harmondsworth: Penguin Books.

Springford, K., & Craig, G. (2001). Review of *Psychoanalysis & Culture; A Kleinian Perspective,* D. Bell (Ed.). *British Journal of Psychotherapy, 18*(1): 137–139.

Sulloway, F. J. (1998). *Born to Rebel.* London: Abacus Books.

Vico, G. (1728). *Autobiography,* T. G. Bergin & M. H. Fisch (Trans.). Ithaca, N.Y.: Cornell University Press, 1963.

Vico, G. (1975). *The New Science* (3rd edn), T. G. Bergin (Ed.) & M. H. Fisch (Trans.). London: Cornell University Press.

Volkan, V. D., & Ast, G. (1997). *Siblings in the Unconscious and Psychopathology.* New York: International Universities Press.

Weeks, R. B. (1976). The sexually exploited Child. *Southern Medical Journal, 69*: 848–852.

Whitehead, C. (1986). The Horus–Osiris cycle: a psychoanalytic investigation. *The International Review of Psycho-Analysis, 13*(1): 77–89.

"The Wolfman" (Pseud.) (1973). Recollections of my childhood. In: M. Gardiner (Ed.), *The Wolfman & Sigmund Freud* (pp. 17–133). U.K.: Penguin Books.

Woof, P. (Ed.) (1991). *The Grasmere Journals: Dorothy Wordsworth.* Oxford: Oxford University Press.

INDEX